THE ROUGH GUIDE to
Running

ROUGH GUIDES

www.roughguides.com

Credits

The Rough Guide to Running

Editors: Sharon Gray, Pat Gilbert
Layout: Fit4Life Media
Picture research: Christopher Lewis/RunCity Images
Proofreading: George Bradley, Erica Parish
Production: Rebecca Short

Rough Guides Reference

Series editor: Mark Ellingham
Editors: Peter Buckley, Duncan Clark,
Tracy Hopkins, Sean Mahoney,
Matthew Milton, Joe Staines, Ruth Tidball
Director: Andrew Lockett

Publishing Information

This first edition published October 2007 by
Rough Guides Ltd, 80 Strand, London WC2R 0RL
345 Hudson St, 4th Floor, New York 10014, USA
Email: mail@roughguides.com

Distributed by the Penguin Group:
Penguin Books Ltd, 80 Strand, London WC2R 0RL
Penguin Putnam, Inc., 375 Hudson Street, NY 10014, USA
Penguin Group (Australia), 250 Camberwell Road, Camberwell, Victoria 3124, Australia
Penguin Books Canada Ltd, 90 Eglinton Avenue East, Suite 700, Toronto, Ontario, Canada, M4P 2YE
Penguin Group (New Zealand), Cnr Rosedale and Airborne Roads, Albany, Auckland, New Zealand

Printed in Italy by LegoPrint S.p.A

Typeset in Minion and Myriad

A catalogue record for this book is available from the British Library

ISBN 13: 978-1-84353-909-4
ISBN 10: 1-84353-909-8

1 3 5 7 9 8 6 4 2

THE ROUGH GUIDE to

Running

by
Lloyd Bradley

Contents

contents

Acknowledgements

The author would like to thank the following, without whom this book would not have been possible: Steve Seaton, Alison Hamlett and Rob "Mr December" Spedding (see p.4) and all at *Runner's World* magazine circa 2003/2004; all at Fit4Life Media and RunCity; Derek Yates, Christopher Lewis, Erica Parish, Sharon Gray and Pat Gilbert; Hugh, Effie, Karen and Barrie, aka *The Rough Guide To Running*'s panel of experts; Ruth Tidball, Andrew Lockett and Peter Buckley; Joel Chernin, Tyrone Whyte and Graham Greig; Simon Kanter, Paul Simpson and Mark Ellingham; Diana, George and Elissa Bradley and all runners everywhere.

Picture credits

All photographs of runners supplied and taken by Steven Seaton; except pp.8, 15, 186 and 238, supplied by RunCity Images.

All still life supplied by RunCity Images; except pp.129 & 196 supplied by DK Images.

Other photos supplied by RunCity Images (pp. 23, 141, 248 and 251); DK Images (pp. 81, 82, 86, 131 and 132).

All illustrations and graphics drawn and supplied by Derek Yates.

Meet the panel

Efua Baker

Previously the resident fitness expert on the BBC's *Fat Nation* and the woman who got Christian Bale into shape for his recent Batman role, former dancer and catwalk model Efua has been a "body sculptor", as she calls it, for over twelve years. Running is at the core of her personal training programmes that involve weights, dance, martial arts, boxing and yoga. "Clients come and ask me 'I want to lose weight, I want to get fit, what should I buy?' I tell them a good pair of running shoes, and that's it!"

Hugh Jones

Hugh Jones won the 1982 London Marathon, setting a British all-comers record of 2:09:24. He represented Britain in the marathon at World Championships and Olympic Games throughout the 1980s, and he has recorded a career total of twelve sub-2:12 marathons. He contributed athletics features to *The Independent* between 1990 and 1994 and has been a regular contributor to *Runner's World* for the last ten years. In 1996 Hugh became the secretary to the Association of International Marathons and Distance Races and the editor of *Distance Running* magazine.

Our panel of experts are, from the left, a fitness instructor, a marathon record breaker, a Grade 3 athletics coach and an osteopath. They have advised us on all aspects of running, recovery and fitness, and have contributed the Expert Advice boxes that appear throughout the book – see right.

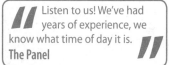

Listen to us! We've had years of experience, we know what time of day it is.
The Panel

Karen Hancock

A Grade 3 athletics coach and Serpentine Running Club stalwart, Karen has represented Scotland in both road and cross-country races. The top-ranked British woman at 20 miles in the 50–54 age group for 2006 and 2nd-ranked at 10 miles, she also won her age-group (45–49) in the Flora London Marathon in 2005. Karen provides marathon training advice for individuals and holds Saturday morning hill sessions in Greenwich. Her coaching philosophy is that distance runners are not born, but made – made out of purposeful training over a number of years.

Barrie Savory D.O.

An osteopath of over 43 years' experience, Barrie was UK Under-19 800 metre champion in 1958, and, more recently, has treated athletes including Seb Coe, Sally Gunnell and Kelly Holmes. Barrie is the author of *The Good Back Guide* (Random House), the authoritative book on the back. It takes the view that our intellectual evolution has outstripped our structural evolution, and as the only animal on the planet that has built its own environment we have become its victim. The foreword was written by HRH Prince Andrew, another of Barrie's clients.

Why run?

Why indeed, when most modern cities have perfectly good cab services?

If the only purpose of running was to get from A to B merely a little bit quicker than you would if you'd walked, a bus would probably serve you better. Equally, there'll be those among you who'll argue that the purpose of running, as a sport, is exactly that – to get from A to B quicker than anybody else.

But to hold either of those views would be to miss the point of why so many millions of us all over the world spend several hours a week running. Often, quite literally, round in circles.

> **"** Most of the people I train are doing it because they want to look good – nobody comes and tells me they want to improve their VO₂ max! And to them that means losing weight. Running is the best exercise there is for burning fat. **"**
> **Efua Baker**

The question to ask really should be "Why not run?"

And if anybody has a good answer to that I've yet to hear it.

Running is one of the simplest, most straightforward and all round effective forms of physical exercise you can take. Pretty much anybody can get into it, as you can start off at your own pace then improve at a rate that suits nobody other than yourself. You don't need a great deal of flashy or expensive kit either, just a pair of shoes and a pair of shorts, although a shirt would be useful. More or less everybody has somewhere to go running; you can do it in a group; or, if you don't want to wait for others, do it by yourself. Plus there aren't any opening hours or membership fees involved.

So there aren't too many excuses not to run that will hold a great deal of water. But if you still need convincing, even in this day and age in which one in four of us is obese and adult onset diabetes is at an all time high, consider this: you won't get hangovers any more. Or if you do they won't be nearly so dreadful. This is because there'll be far less crap floating about in your newly healthy system to start off with; then a runner's highly efficient metabolism quickly gets rid of all those hangover-inducing toxins that will be left behind by a night on the lash.

Plus you'll have been paying much more attention to your hydration during the day – drinking loads of water will have become a habit – so you'll have started off protected against the booze's diuretic side effect, and so sidestep that morning-after thirst.

Yet we're still kind of missing a trick. The biggest trick of all, as well. Running – round the streets, on the beach or through a forest – is one of the most liberating experiences there is. Beyond even the many physical benefits of running, the rush of exhilaration as you charge down a hill or try to beat a bus to the next stop is enough to put a great big grin on even the grumpiest of faces. As well as the "runner's high" of an endorphin rush that could flatten a charging rhino, there's an almost cathartic effect in just you running like a train and coming out triumphant over whatever course or distance or timing you pit yourself against. Go for a good run in the evening and it's as if you sweat out all that day's frustrations and niggles.

Also, in today's hi-tech, handheld, downloadable world there's something satisfyingly pure about succeeding on your own physical merits. When you run, the amount of advantage you can buy, in terms of what you wear or carry, will be so negligible as to make no difference at all. As I said earlier, just shoes and shorts and you can get started, then it's you against yourself and the elements, which is about the best way there is for testing what you're really made of.

Would 130,000 people really have applied for 35,000 places in last year's Flora London Marathon, signing up for six months of gruelling training and the "joy" of slogging 26.2 miles around the capital's streets, if running wasn't all that?

The Rough Guide To Running

This book is all about running. From the celebration of it to the history of it – the Olympic marathon's distance used to be an entirely flexible affair, depending on what was most convenient for

> **//** Running is such an obvious thing to do. When I was a kid I used to run just to get places and back. I don't know if I thought of it as fun, but when I won a Boy Scouts cross-country race against boys much older than myself I realized I was actually quite good at it. **//**
> **Hugh Jones**

the organizer – to how to start off in it, to how to get better at it if you're already doing it, and how to prepare for a marathon.

The first section, **Starting off**, deals with exactly that, starting off, and will offer advice and guidance for those who have never run further than for a bus. In three detailed chapters it'll take you from your sofa to a respectable time for a 5k in a matter of weeks. While it does so, it'll help you get a grip on what you should be eating

and drinking in order to make this happen as easily as possible. Those important periods immediately before and after your run are covered, so as to lessen the chance of injury and help you recover with a minimum of discomfort. The section also picks through that potential minefield that is running kit, pointing out what you *don't* need as well as what you do.

One foot in front of the other, the second section, assumes you're no longer a novice, and is all about improving your running and increasing your confidence while you're putting in the miles. Separate chapters cover the actual biomechanics of running and the internal workings of the powerplant that is your heart, lungs and metabolism, discussing what you can do to get the greatest results for the most energy-conserving effort. This takes on much of the theory, explaining the "why" in order for you to get much more out of the "what". This section also discusses training techniques and how to measure your improvements, but, of equal importance, there's a comprehensive chapter on injuries and another on staying safe while out on a run. Not that this is meant to put you off, but if you want a long running life you're going to have to look after yourself.

The final section is **Running for real** – we thought about calling it Running 4 real, then went for a long run and realized that was just plain daft. It's about what you do with your running now you've got it, and will set you up for those first races and fun runs, providing a list of the best events the UK has to offer. Then in spite of running being one of the most egalitarian of sports, there are bits of it that don't apply to everybody so this section contains chapters specifically for the older runner and for women. And as some sort of finale, there's the chapter on marathon running, complete with training schedules that should take you from 10k to the big 26.2.

In the margins throughout the book are tips and facts that provide knowledge bursts to give you an added edge, offer short cuts to running enlightenment or might just make you smile. Also down the sides of the pages are nuggets of insider advice on all aspects of running from our esteemed panel of experts – two renowned runners, one a former Flora London Marathon record holder; a TV fitness coach; and Prince Andrew's osteopath. They offer a range of specialist knowledge that you won't find in any other running book. This is a unique and enormously valuable opportunity to learn from those who genuinely know, and you'll do well to pay special attention to those boxes with the quotation marks in them. Once again, ladies and gentlemen, give it up for Hugh Jones, Efua Baker, Karen Hancock and Barrie Savory, *The Rough Guide To Running*'s panel of experts.

Enjoy your run.

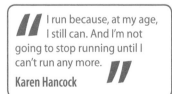

I run because, at my age, I still can. And I'm not going to stop running until I can't run any more.

Karen Hancock

Getting started

Starting off

Your first run will probably be the most difficult run you'll ever do.

And not just because your muscles will be working overtime to cope with what you're putting them through.

Although running is, theoretically, one of the least complicated or involved of all fitness activities, if you want to get the most out of it without doing yourself damage, there is actually a fair amount you need to know. As such, taking on board all the well-meaning advice you'll receive (astonishingly, as much from non-runners as runners) and working out what aspects of running will be best for you so often puts people off before they start. And then you've still got to get past the embarrassment factor and the self-motivational bit.

This first chapter should answer all your initial questions and give the sort of guidance you need to make sure you start your running experience as efficiently and as safely as possible. It will even offer a few tips to get you out of that front door.

Should I be running?

Of course you should.

As regards whether or not you are healthy enough to take up running as an activity, the simple answer is yes. Probably. Although, increasingly, the trend is to assume you might not be.

Before anybody starts any exercise programme or takes up any vigorous sport they should get a thorough check-up from their GP. Or at least that's the theory in a world gripped tight by rear-end-covering advice from Health & Safety Overkill. The pragmatic truth is that, unless you are worried about a pre-existing condition or something in your medical history, you shouldn't need your doctor's permission to take up running. Indeed, if you visit your doctor simply to ask whether you should hit the pavements or not and manage to get to the surgery under your own steam, they are going to wonder why you are wasting their time. The chances are they couldn't give you much guidance anyway.

The average family doctor isn't going to know enough about running and how beginners actually get started in it to make an informed judgement based on anything other than obvious conditions. Such are the pressures on the modern health service, preventative measures or health'n'fitness consultation no longer seem part of what they do, as they have become geared up to treat illness and ailments *after* the event. This isn't an attack on family doctors – they mostly do a sterling job given the circumstances. It's merely a reflection on their workload and the average six-minutes-per-patient visit. Thus they are highly unlikely to appreciate an apparently healthy person taking up their time to ask "Should I take up a cardio-vascular exercise and get out in the fresh air more?"

Think of the time spent hanging round the doctor's surgery as time when you could be out running, and only book that appointment

Tip: If you're still worried about your fitness to run, you could give NHS Direct (0845 4647) a call or ask for guidance or even a fitness test at your local gym.

Fact: If you are on a low-carb diet – Atkins, for instance – you shouldn't be running. Without the carbohydrates necessary to maintain the energy levels you'll need for running, this sort of prolonged exercise could be very dangerous (see p.30).

if you have specific grounds for hesitancy – see box below. And as regards being fit, people take up running in order to get fit, so if you had to be a perfect physical specimen in order to partake, most of us would have been excluded. The trick is to start slowly – and we mean *slowly*. For the reasonably healthy, if you follow the beginners' programmes (see pp.18–19) and listen to your body as soon as it starts complaining, you will be fine.

See your doctor before taking up running if:

You are over 60

You are already under a doctor's care for an existing condition

You or your family has a history of heart problems

You are asthmatic

You are on medication

You have had an adverse reaction to exercise in the past

You have arthritis

You have uncontrollable high blood pressure

Will I look stupid?

No. Of course you won't. Not unless you're running a marathon dressed as a carrot, and then it'll probably be deliberate. But that doesn't mean you won't *feel* like you look stupid during your first few times on the street, and that's what counts.

In spite of what you might imagine, as you pound the pavements wearing not much more than your underwear, the reality is that most people won't even have noticed you. Just put your head down – not literally, in case you

Tip: If you decide to get checked out first, it is better to go and see a doctor who specializes in sports medicine and understands the process of becoming a runner. Try Yellow Pages or your local athletics club for names.

If you are serious about running, make sure your machine is at its optimum operating efficiency. Before problems arise, check out with a podiatrist if there is any doubt over your pronation (see p.44). Similarly, check out your spine and pelvic mechanics with a suitable and athletically knowledgable therapist. It is always cheaper to prevent than to cure.
Barrie Savory D.O.

Tip: The best way to react to a van driver's "jovial" shouts of "Run, Forrest, run!" is with a few yards of comedy-style running – ramrod-straight back, energetically pumping arms, and knees lifted above waist height.

Tip: If you are using a watch with a digital second counter to measure your pulse, try not to stare at it throughout the minute, because you will end up counting seconds rather than pulse beats.

run into a tree, then people really will notice you – and power on through. After a few times out you will feel much more in command of your actual running, thus you'll be more confident, and will realize you have much more important things to think about than pedestrians you might pass. Just keep telling yourself how much longer you are going to live than them.

How fit am I and how fit will I become?

Your own personal fitness when you start running will depend on a number of contributing factors: your age; your exercise history; whether you do an active or a sedentary job; whether you are a smoker or not. How fit you are when you take up running need not make a difference to what you will be able to achieve on the road, but it will affect how easily your body adapts to the demands of a runner's training schedule. Therefore, it can help you determine at which level to hurl yourself into training.

The most reliable method for finding out how fit you are, without leaving the comfort of your own home, is to measure your resting heart rate – that's your heart rate while you are not, or have not recently been, exerting yourself. If you haven't got a heart-rate monitor, find the pulse in your radial artery by lightly resting your middle and index fingers at the base of your thumb, just below the wrist. The fitter you are, the lower your resting heart rate will be.

Even if you're fit enough to run marathons, you're not invincible. Stuff that is bad for you will still be bad for you, it's just that you'll be in better shape to cope with the things that will do you harm.
Karen Hancock

Beats per minute	Level of fitness	In running terms
80–100	Unfit	Absolute beginner
70–80	UK average	Should cope with first phase (see p.18)
50–70	Fit	Should take to running with ease
30–50	Extremely fit	Do you already run marathons?

It is impossible to predict how fit you will become as you progress as a runner because everybody's capacities will be different, and

Body Mass Index

Another indicator of the shape you are in is the Body Mass Index. It was devised in the mid-nineteenth century to measure as a single figure how overweight people were, accounting for their height. To achieve your BMI, divide your weight in kilogrammes by the square of your height in metres, then apply the figure to the chart below. In spite of BMI becoming much talked about in the current obesity crisis, it is a relatively crude measurement and does not recognize gender, race or muscle mass.

Body Mass Index	Weight Status
Below 17	Possible malnutrition
17.1–18.5	Underweight
18.6–25	Normal
25.1–30	Overweight
30.1–40	Obese
Over 40	Morbidly obese

BMI calculator

$$\frac{\text{weight (kg)}}{\text{height (m) x height (m)}}$$

Or, if maths isn't your thing, you can use the online calculator at:
www.nhlbisupport.com/bmi

could vary as their situation changes. Suffice to say, as a runner you will be fitter than you were before you took up the sport. As you train and your running improves, you should regularly take your resting heart rate and keep a record, in order to measure your fitness level as it increases. When you take your heart rate for your records, always do so at the same time of day because your heart will be working at different rates throughout an average day.

How far should I run to start off with?

The biggest consideration at this point is to get your muscles used to exercise and, even if you are fairly active already, to maintaining aerobic effort over a period of time. In the beginning you should

Tip: If you are running with somebody else, use the "talk test" to judge if your speed is correct: if you are too breathless to conduct a conversation you are probably running too fast.

Slow down. That's the advice I give to all my clients who tell me they can't run for more than five minutes. It's because so many new runners start off as if it was a sprint and collapse after about five hundred metres.
Efua Baker

measure your running by the minute rather than by the mile. When you start, you'll find your own pace and then increase your stamina by building up longer periods of time between rests. Once you're running for about 15 minutes at a time you should be covering around two kilometres and then you can start talking in distances.

Unless you are chronically unfit, begin with a session of around half an hour, alternating very short periods of running and walking. This might not seem very exciting, or even particularly athletic, but this is exactly how slowly the previously mentioned "starting slowly" has to be. The idea is to gently ease your body into an activity that, up until now, has been totally alien to it – and to do so in a way that will result in the least amount of discomfort. It's important to remember that *any* amount of extra exercise will cause you some pain in your muscles afterwards. This is unavoidable but it is vital you keep this to a minimum when starting out, for both physical and psychological reasons. The more soreness you experience, the longer your recovery time needs to be, and if you have to wait several days between exercise schedules at this stage you will not build up any strength and will effectively be starting from scratch every time. Also, if it hurts too much you are less likely to do it again.

First phase training schedule

This suggested training schedule assumes just a basic level of fitness – ie you can walk briskly for around 15 minutes. None of this is set in stone though, as everybody will find a different level as soon as they start. If, after the first week, you are sure you are not being pushed hard enough, feel free to skip forward on the chart.

Each session includes five minutes' walking to warm up; on the sessions that end with running add five minutes of brisk walking to cool down. When sessions call for walking, do not walk too slowly and allow your body to cool down. The schedules call for three sessions per week, with at least one rest day in between. You will need a stopwatch or a robust watch with a second hand.

Week no.	Session 1	Session 2	Session 3
One	Five minutes brisk walking to warm up Run one minute Walk one minute Repeat 10 times 25-minute session 10 minutes running	Five minutes brisk walking to warm up Run one minute Walk one minute Repeat 10 times 25-minute session 10 minutes running	Five minutes brisk walking to warm up Run one minute Walk one minute Repeat 10 times 25-minute session 10 minutes running
Two	Five minutes brisk walking to warm up Run two minutes Walk two minutes Repeat five times 25-minute session 10 minutes running	Five minutes brisk walking to warm up Run two minutes Walk two minutes Repeat five times 25-minute session 10 minutes running	Five minutes brisk walking to warm up Run three minutes Walk three minutes Repeat four times 29-minute session 12 minutes running
Three	Five minutes brisk walking to warm up Run three minutes Walk three minutes Repeat four times 29-minute session 12 minutes running	Five minutes brisk walking to warm up Run three minutes Walk three minutes Repeat four times 29-minute session 12 minutes running	Five minutes brisk walking to warm up Run four minutes Walk three minutes Repeat four times 33-minute session 16 minutes running
Four	Five minutes brisk walking to warm up Run five minutes Walk three minutes Repeat three times 29-minute session 15 minutes running	Five minutes brisk walking to warm up Run five minutes Walk two minutes Repeat four times 33-minute session 20 minutes running	Five minutes brisk walking to warm up Run seven minutes Walk three minutes Repeat four times 45-minute session 28 minutes running

Walk before you run

If you have led an utterly inactive life up to now or you are very overweight, you will need to start your running programme by walking. Just walk for about 10 minutes at a quicker-than-average pace – you'll need to break sweat but not become breathless. Rest for two to three minutes, then briskly walk for another 10 minutes. Do this three times a week for two weeks, with at least one rest day in between each exercise day, and gradually increase your walking pace or add five minutes to the time. After a fortnight, you should be ready to take on the First Phase running programme outlined left.

// When I start people off who have never run before I get them to "Walk a lamppost, run a lamppost" then as they build up stamina and fitness I move them up to "Walk a lamppost run two lampposts". And we progress from there to run them all. //
Efua Baker

Second phase training schedule

If you can already run for around 15 minutes, or have completed the previous schedule, the following will be suited to your level. After you have completed this phase, you should be ready to finish a 5k race in a respectable time (see p.205) and will definitely have reached the point at which you can plan your own runs, and do so as much by distance as time.

Week no.	Session 1	Session 2	Session 3
One	Five minutes brisk walking to warm up Run seven minutes Walk two minutes Repeat three times Run five minutes 42-minute session 26 minutes running	Five minutes brisk walking to warm up Run eight minutes Walk three minutes Repeat three times Run five minutes 48-minute session 29 minutes running	Five minutes brisk walking to warm up Run 20 minutes nonstop 30-minute session 20 minutes running
Two	Five minutes brisk walking to warm up Run 10 minutes Walk two minutes Repeat three times 41-minute session 30 minutes running	Five minutes brisk walking to warm up Run 10 minutes Walk two minutes Repeat three times Run five minutes 51-minute session 35 minutes running	Five minutes brisk walking to warm up Run 25 minutes nonstop 35-minute session 25 minutes running
Three	Five minutes brisk walking to warm up Run 15 minutes Walk two minutes Repeat three times 56-minute session 45 minutes running	Five minutes brisk walking to warm up Run 15 minutes Walk two minutes Repeat three times 56-minute session 45 minutes running	Five minutes brisk walking to warm up Run 30 minutes nonstop 40-minute session 30 minutes running

When should I run?

It's tempting to say "whenever you get a spare half hour!" but that approach would be too random. The most common excuse for not going running – or doing any sort of exercise – is not having the time, so the best way around that is to settle on a regular time and incorporate it into your daily routine. For instance, 30 minutes between 6.30 and 7am on weekdays and one hour from 9 to 10am at weekends. Or, you could try running every other lunchtime or running home from work. Once it becomes a regular fixture, it will simply be one more thing you do, almost mundane, and not something you have to think about, or do your best to put off. Also, your body will thank you for the regularity as the punishment you'll be meting out will become part of its routine too, and it will be better prepared to cope with it.

> I find the best time to run is first thing in the morning. As the day goes on you'll be able to find more and more reasons why not to. Also, whatever else you do or don't do that day, you've still been running.
> **Karen Hancock**

Where should I run?

Not all distance running is the same. Different aspects make varying demands on the runner and, understandably, offer up dissimilar rewards and benefits. The chances are you will settle on road running – around seventy per cent of the UK's runners run exclusively on pavement – but before you make your choice you should understand what the possibilities are.

Track running

This is so close to road running that you won't need any special equipment or technique to cope with it other than, perhaps, a phenomenally high boredom threshold. The only real difference between the two is that modern running tracks are softer than pavements and so will be more forgiving on your joints. Don't believe the myth that if you run round a track in the same direction all the time, leaning into the bends, you'll develop one leg much

Fact: Track running is slightly faster than road running. Don't be fooled into thinking you've made a miraculous improvement if you run a quicker 5k on the big red oval.

Tip: Splay your feet slightly when running on very wet ground as this will help to stop you slipping. Don't run like this more than you have to though, as it is incredibly energy inefficient.

stronger than the other. Most tracks are 400m ovals with relatively gentle curved ends, and the speed you'll be going through them will mean you shouldn't be anything other than upright.

Cross-country running

Cross-country can be dangerous and exhausting, putting you at the mercy of the elements and covering you in mud, but at the same time it can give you a fantastic running experience with huge mental and physical benefits. If you run a route that takes you through woods and across streams as well as open fields, it's easy to pretend you're in a battle with nature. Then, if you get soaked, muddy and maybe even a little bloody, you really will feel like some sort of warrior. It is also totally unpredictable, and even your regular route will be noticeably different each time you run it. Cross-country is enormously exhilarating and about the most fun you can have with your running shoes on.

Leaving aside its obvious perils – slipping over, being chased or attacked by animals, running into trees, dodging lightning, brambles or weirdos in woods and so on – you should relish the fact that you will gain more from it physically than road running because pushing off from an uneven surface constantly alters the angles of your legs, which requires a greater range of muscles to be used. In addition, because good cross-country running employs a shorter stride to cope more effectively with soft and slippery ground, it has less elastic recoil and therefore causes you to develop more power in the hips and thighs – cross-country runners tend to do well in road races because of this added strength. Also, running on softer surfaces removes much of the stress on leg joints that comes from road running.

Be aware of safety when cross-country running – solitude may be beautiful but you will be alone if something goes wrong

Trail running

Running through forests or parks on prescribed paths of bark chips or wood mulch is already widespread in America, and is becoming increasingly popular in the UK as more and more woodlands are opened to the public and nature trails are put down. Trail running has got a reputation as "cross-country for wimps", simply because public Health & Safety requirements mean that these pathways have to avoid so many of nature's inherent hazards. But take no notice of such talk. Although trail running might not be sufficiently taxing for the real hard-core runners, for the rest of

us it is about as perfect a situation as anybody could hope for. You are close to nature, but it's nature that's managed to such a degree it's not scary at all – for that reason personal safety is much greater. Also most woodlands are far more interesting than most streets, you are removed from traffic hazards and pollution, and the prepared surface will have enough cushion to make it easy on your knees and ankles, but not so much give as to work against you.

Road running

The vast majority of you will do nothing other than road running in your entire running life, and for this reason it is the Ground Zero

Calorie counter

Surface	Calorific consumption
Cross-country	Extremely high
Beach	Very high
Trail	High
Road	High
Track	Medium
Treadmill	Low

Most treadmills can be adjusted to increase the work rate.

of running – the yardstick by which other forms are judged. It's the one we're referring to in this book when we simply talk about "running", and it's what nearly all running shoes are designed to cope with. In fact, unless you specify otherwise, you will be sold road-running shoes.

Beach running

If you are lucky enough to live near a sandy beach, run on it at every opportunity! You'll feel so much better as the sea air will do your lungs the world of good, while the sight, sound and smell of the waves is a marvellous psychological boost. Running on soft sand will give you a good workout too, as the unevenness and the lack of traction means you'll have to work that bit harder to dig your feet out of it and cover the distance – in fact you should shorten your stride slightly to counteract the yielding surface.

Many runners prefer running on the packed sand at the water's edge for a firmer push, even dodging in and out of waves. Fun as this might be, squelchy running shoes aren't, so it's not recommended if you have to travel a long way in them after your run. While running on sand will be far more forgiving if you are recovering

from an injury, try to avoid beaches with steep cambers as you will naturally try to keep your body vertical and in doing so put added strain on your ankles, knees and hips.

Tip: Don't be tempted to run barefoot on the beach as they often have variable surfaces and your feet and ankles need all the support they can get.

Fact: Don't worry about timings if you're running on a beach; under these circumstances they will always be slow.

Type of running	Pros	Cons
Cross-country	Brings you close to nature; more intense muscular workout; never boring; soft surface; solitude	Treacherous under foot; dangerous obstacles; unnerving detachment from civilization
Beach running	Invigorating environment; very fresh air; increased calorie burning; soft surface	Beach camber can damage lower joints; no hills
Trail running	Brings you close to nature but in a managed environment; soft surface	Opening hours; can get crowded
Road running	Everybody has access to a road system; route is infinitely variable in length or difficulty; no awkward opening hours.	Pavement jars knees and ankles; potential danger from traffic or assault; pollution
Track running	Safe; slightly faster; softer surface than road running; changing rooms	Boring; prohibitive opening hours; can get crowded
Treadmill	You can watch TV; all-weather access; accurately measurable; adjustable for effort required; not in public; cushioned to reduce impact on joints	Soul-destroyingly dull; seemingly pointless; difficult to sustain for a long spell; little chance of privacy; might affect your balance

Tip: Purpose-built rubber shock absorption mats to go under the treadmill can be bought for around £50, and are a worthwhile investment if your machine is noisy.

Treadmill running

There is a great deal of disparaging stuff said about how boring and "unreal" treadmill running is, and while most of this is true, these drawbacks are vastly outweighed by the advantages.

Any sort of running is better than no running at all, and for many novices the treadmill at their gym is where they feel most confident and relaxed about it. You will never be held slave to the weather on a treadmill, you shouldn't have to worry too much about personal safety, what time of the day (or night!) it is will be less of an issue, then there's what some may consider quite a bonus – you can watch TV as you run. Even if a noisy, crowded gym is not to your taste, the range of home-use treadmills on offer will accommodate most budgets (see panel opposite).

Prolonged treadmill running may affect your stride, as it lengthens foot drag which will have to be compensated for in your balance, but the real disadvantage with it lies in what you'll be missing out on. So many of the reasons why many of us took up running in the first place will be lost: fresh air (even the most crowed cities are breathable in the early mornings); inspiration from your surroundings; and the motivation to carry on running for another couple of hours.

Should I run by myself or with a friend?

As every runner has a different reason for being out there pounding the pavements, there are no prescribed guidelines about whether you should go running by yourself or not. With the exception of my time at *Runner's World* magazine, I make it a point to run by myself – it's possibly the best "me time" there is as you're alone with your thoughts, in the fresh air, working your system to send increased blood and oxygen to your brain, surrounded by nature (on about half of my runs) and doing something you can feel smugly

How to buy a treadmill

A domestic-use treadmill could cost anything between £200 and £2,000, and for runners rather than walkers it will be at the more expensive end of the market as we need stronger motors, more efficient shock absorption and bigger tread areas.

You will need a floor area of roughly 3 x 1.5 metres when it's operational, and a bigger storage space than you might think, even if it folds up. Look for what continuous duty horsepower (chp) the motor offers – ignore the peak duty figure – and make sure it's at least 2.5chp. Your stride will require a minimum tread area of 1.3 x 0.5 metres, and a maximum user weight of between 120 to 130kgs means the unit can take quite a bashing. The top speed should be more than 17kph, and the incline needs to be motorised and go up to at least 10 per cent.

Shock absorption is very important, especially if it is going to be used on a wooden floor or where other people live underneath – remember, when you try treadmills out, the chances are they will be on carpeted concrete floors. Look for a machine with dampening under the deck (the rigid platform the belt wraps around). The more expensive models will have a cushioned deck, which will be as kind to your joints as it is to the folk downstairs.

The most important aspect of the display panel is an easily accessible emergency stop button – remarkably, not every model has one. The readouts you need are speed, distance covered and time, and if it has an incline facility it should display the angle. Most treadmills will offer a calories burnt counter, but this will not be overly precise as everybody burns calories at different rates. Heart-rate monitors are common too, but if you already own one (see p.64) don't pay extra for one built in to your treadmill.

righteous about. Other people, however, will use running as time spent together, or appreciate the banter and mutual encouragement of running as a group or in tandem.

When you start out as a runner, the advantages of going out with a running buddy – either a fellow novice or an experienced runner – will vastly outweigh the joys of solitude. Quite apart from having somebody to talk to, not being by yourself will reduce your very natural feelings of self-consciousness as you step outside your front door wearing brand new running kit. You'll either be distracted from thinking everybody's staring at you, not worry so much because there are two of you, or simply assume people are gawping at whoever it is swaddled in Lycra and running next to you! Also, you will feel far less vulnerable. This is very important, as you won't have too much on and it takes a bit of getting used to before you will relax into it – until then you will feel much more secure if you are not going through this by yourself.

Your running will benefit enormously too, and it will be much easier to stick to schedules if you are running with somebody else, or if an experienced runner is coaching you. A friendly rivalry as you start to get better will do wonders for your progress, as will being urged along by a seasoned runner. In the latter case, problems can be worked out immediately; should you injure yourself – and beginners are much more likely to – there will be someone there to help, and you'll be able to discuss any thoughts you have about your running with somebody who can see what's going on. Also, it will be much harder to skip a session if your running buddy is performing stretches on your front path!

How do I motivate myself?

So much of running is in the mind – going through The Wall; putting on that little spurt; carrying on for another 20 minutes; and

Fact: It's usually easy for beginners to find an experienced runner to run with, just ask around – few runners will refuse. And don't worry about irritating an old hand by running slowly; we've all been beginners and (in most cases) somebody else took time to help us.

not least, getting out there in the beginning. Because you won't yet have experienced running's highs, your motivation to actually get started needs to be powerful, but if you've come this far – ie either bought this book or stood in the shop for a long time reading it – then you're more than halfway to getting out there.

Spending a couple of hundred pounds on running kit is usually a strong force to tip you out of that armchair, and so is embarrassment. Shame yourself into actually starting by buying a big calendar, hanging it up in a prominent place, then colouring in every day you put off going for that first run! Really though, this is your chance to flex one of your body's strongest muscles – your brain – and simply will yourself off that sofa and into a running routine. There's no way it can be as bad as you think it might be.

Five tricks to get you out of the front door

1. Get changed into your running kit. It will put you in a running frame of mind, and, fairly quickly, it will be easier to go for a run than have everybody else in the house ask "You going for a run then?"

2. Arrange for a running buddy to call for you. Then you can't get out of it, or you'll have wasted their time, too.

3. Have a stretch. You'll release endorphins that will make you feel much livelier, and your newly loosened muscles will start nagging you to hit the road.

4. The 20-minute rule. If you think you really don't feel like a long run, promise yourself you'll only do 20 minutes. Once you hit that mark and you're properly warmed up, you'll want to carry on for ever.

5. Read the TV schedules. When you confront yourself with the Three Rs – reality, repeats and rubbish – you'll start running just to get away from your set.

> I can remember hearing the rain on the window and thinking it was far worse out there than it really was, so you just have to remember how much better you'll feel when you're running. It's the thought of getting wet rather than the actual getting wet that's the problem.
> **Hugh Jones**

Fact: Your body will tell you what it needs, and as you start building up your running schedule, you will find yourself wanting more bread, pasta or porridge, foods you may not have liked much previously but which your body knows will provide it with the right carbohydrate.

Diet and when you eat before you run is so much down to the individual. Although a book like this is a very useful guideline, you have to experiment and try out different things to find what works best for you.
Efua Baker

Tip: When planning your runner's diet, be aware that many high-protein foods – meat and dairy – are also high in saturated fat.

What should I eat?

Once you take up any form of exercise on a regular basis, you will need to change your diet because the demands being made on your system for fuel and muscle growth will be very different from what was needed to power your old sedentary lifestyle. As regards running, it's not so much a question of specific foods as two basic rules: 1) dump the junk; and 2) increase the carbs.

Getting rid of processed food is an obvious step, because so little of it contains any nutrients and the sugar content of so much of it will mess with your energy levels. Your body eats, primarily, to nourish itself, and when it needs more nutrients it will make you feel hungry. The problem with junk food is, because it is of so little nutritional value, you need more sooner rather than later. Once you start regular running and your metabolic rate speeds up, the amount of junk food you would need will increase exponentially. This can mean that, even though you are exercising regularly, you might still put on weight.

So much processed food has a high sugar content – not just cakes and sweets – and as a simple carbohydrate, a concentrated quantity of sugar will do your running no good. It will cause sudden spikes in the glucose level in your blood stream, and the resultant energy rush will be followed very quickly by the sort of crash that can leave you feeling weak and pretty miserable. Too much sugar at one time can also deplete your energy supplies, which will be diverted into breaking the sugar down, and it can inhibit your system's ability to absorb fluid (see p.36).

Although there will be times when a controlled short-term boost from sugar may be useful on a long distance run, as a beginner it's best to stay away from excesses of it as part of your eating plan.

You don't need to completely ignore the sweet trolley though – getting around 15 per cent of your carbohydrate intake from sugar will do you no harm. However, try to avoid refined white sugar – factory-produced confectionery and cakes will be full of it – and get most of your simple carbs from fresh fruit or juice, as they will have a decent nutrient content as well.

The carbs a regular runner needs in his or her diet are the complex carbohydrates – starches – found in products such as wholewheat pasta and bread, in whole cereals, potatoes, rice and fresh vegetables. These carbohydrates are vital as they are a runner's primary source of energy and are absorbed into your system slowly, thus providing an evenly paced, long-term fuel supply to your muscles, which will keep you going much longer (see p.113). This is why, if you are running to lose weight, you cannot do it on diets like Atkins or South Beach – these eating plans are a runner's worst nightmare, as they all but cut out the carbs and will not provide the energy you need to run more than a few yards.

Tip: Vegetarian runners need to make particularly sure they are getting enough iron and that it is being used to its maximum. Vegetarian iron (non-heme iron, found in veg, fruit and cereal) will be better absorbed if consumed with vitamin C, and not within an hour of a cup of tea or coffee as caffeine blocks iron absorption.

Don't eat too late!
You shouldn't eat a heavy meal less that two hours before you go for a run. However, a carb "top up" of a piece of fruit or a sports drink just before you set off will repay later in terms of energy reserves.

Fact: The complex carbohydrates you need to power up your running can also be great sources of fibre, which will work wonders in keeping your digestive system healthy and ensure you are getting all the nutrients out of the food you are eating.

> **"** Stay away from fad diets. Your body will tell you what you need, and if you listen to it you won't go very wrong. **"**
>
> **Hugh Jones**

Fact: For a healthy, balanced diet, 85 per cent of the carbs you eat should be complex and two thirds of the fat should be polyunsaturated or monosaturated.

Fact: Despite the bad reputation butter has gained over recent years, healthwise, there isn't a great deal to choose from between it and margarine. Margarine will be made from healthier unsaturated fats, but there is also a chance it will be hydrogenated, a chemical process that hardens natural oils and carries so many health risks it cancels out most of margarine's cholesterol-lowering benefits. All hydrogenated fats should be avoided.

Taking on huge amounts of carbohydrates won't be just part of your everyday eating plan either. On long runs, you will need to take on carbs as you are running (see p.35) and when you are finished, your body will crave a big bowl of pasta to restock your glycogen levels.

Standard healthy diet	50% carbs, 20% protein, 30% fat
Runner's diet	60–65% carbs, 15% protein, 20–25% fat
Typical low-carb diet	40% carbs, 30% protein, 30% fat

Increasing your carbohydrate intake will be at the expense of fat and protein, both of which tend to make up too much of the modern Western diet. Fat is necessary as a partial energy supply and a huge source of flavour – any diet needs to be something you *want* to eat, rather than something to be endured – but you should be careful about what sort of fat. Saturated fats, mostly from animal sources such as red meat and dairy, should be avoided as much as possible as they will raise Low Density Lipoprotein (LDL) cholesterol (the "bad" artery-clogging, heart-attack-inducing kind) in your bloodstream. Polyunsaturated and monosaturated fats – most plant oils and fish oils – however, can actually counteract that harmful cholesterol by raising levels of "good" High Density Lipoprotein (HDL) in your bloodstream. You should try to regulate your fat intake to two thirds polyunsaturated/monosaturated and one third saturated fat.

Protein is vital for muscle rebuilding and repair, but although you will be increasing your exercise rate therefore putting more stress on your muscles, you have to monitor your protein intake carefully. Any excess of protein not used for building – and the modern diet contains too much protein in general – will be converted to fat to be either burnt as energy or stored, and as you will be meeting your energy needs with carbs it will be turned into fat. Excess protein will also put added strain on your kidneys, meaning they will require more water passing through them in order to function properly, and when out on a run this can lead to dehydration as it will divert fluid from your body's cooling system.

Energy bars

Because a distance runner's energy metabolisation is a continuous process (see p.113), on any run longer than a couple of hours you will need to refuel en route, and energy bars present an easy option. There are so many on the market now, and while all will provide some sort of calorific boost – around 250 calories in a 75g bar – how they do it can vary enormously. The best bars for you as a runner should contain around 50 per cent carbohydrate, which is where the energy comes from, 10 per cent protein to assist with muscle repair and rebuilding, and about 12 per cent soluble fibre. Of the carbohydrate, around half should come from sugar and this ought to be provided by dried fruit within the bar. Whole grain should make up the rest. Always read the ingredients of bars you haven't tried before, try and opt for natural ingredients and stay away from those with many artificial ingredients or a high proportion of sugar.

Although today's energy bars are tailored for the sports market and present a portable, enticingly flavoured, maybe enriched, unmeltable calorie supply, they are relatively expensive. Other energy sources such as bananas, chocolate or cereal bars can provide far more calories for your money – runners and cyclists I know will entertain nothing other than Jaffa Cakes for their energy fixes during a race – they are made up of 67 per cent carbs (nearly all sugar), five per cent protein, two per cent fibre and 0.1 per cent sodium, since you ask…

> As you get more intense about your running, you'll probably find the length of time between when you eat and when you run increases, so don't be a slave to the idea of two hours before.
> **Efua Baker**

Tip: Don't assume you can miss meals and scoff down energy bars instead of proper food. Although some might give you a sugar rush to get you through those last couple of hours of the day, they will not provide enough of what you need nutritionally.

What should I drink?

Hydration, hydration, hydration are the runner's three most important rules, and it's not simply a matter of taking a drink when you feel thirsty.

Tip: On a long run, drink small amounts of water often, as although you may need 800ml of fluids per hour, few people's systems could cope with that amount all in one go. If you try and drink that much water, it could lead to uncomfortable bloating and a rapid discharge of urine.

Tip: To find the fluid loss as a percentage of your body weight, divide the difference between your pre- and post-run weights by your pre-run weight (all converted into ounces) and multiply the result by 100.

Even on a cold day you will get warm when you run, because the body's optimum temperature for energy exploitation is 102–103°F (38.8–39.5°C), a few degrees above normal. As a result, you will start to sweat to cool yourself off and perspiration combined with moisture exhalation, which also increases as you exert yourself, quickly depletes your fluid levels. If you are left with nothing to sweat, you will quickly start to dehydrate and overheat, which can lead to an accelerated heart rate, muscle cramps, headaches and fatigue, hugely impairing your performance (see chart opposite). You will need to be well-hydrated before you start your run and, if it is a long one, to take on fluids during it.

Don't follow your thirst. This is a notoriously unhelpful indicator of when you need to take on fluids, simply because by the time you feel thirsty you are already dehydrated and your performance and concentration levels are heading south. Make sure you have had plenty to drink before your run by drinking 500ml of water between one and two hours before you set out, then top it up with 250ml with around 15 minutes to go. Your urine will be a good indication of your hydration levels – if it is clear you are sufficiently watered.

During your run you will need to take on fluids at between 250ml and 350ml every 15 minutes to avoid dehydration, and even higher amounts in hot weather or if your perspiration rate (see box on p.37) is particularly high. Start your fluid intake after the first 15 minutes and then keep drinking at regular intervals because it is much easier for your body to keep on a hydrated level than to have to get back to one after getting dehydrated. If you are on a long run,

The effects of dehydration

By taking the discrepancy between pre-run and post-run weight (without factoring in fluid consumed) you can work out how much you have dehydrated. Then calculate that figure as a percentage of your body weight, apply it to the chart, and you'll be able to see how your performance may have been affected by dehydration.

% Body Weight Lost	Stage	Symptoms	Effect
1–2%	Normal	None	Shouldn't affect performance
2–3%	Initial stages of dehydration	Thirst	Reduced VO$_2$ max
3–4%	Dehydration starting to tell	Dry mouth	Reduced endurance
4–5%	Aerobic ability impaired	All over discomfort	Running seems much harder
5–6%	Body temperature rising	Increased heart rate and breathing	Slowing down of pace; decision making impaired
6–7%	Body temperature rising dangerously	Cardiovascular rates continue to rise; hot flushes;	Loss of balance; headache; dizziness
7–8%	Blood thickening due to lack of oxygen in system	Difficulty breathing	Total weakness
8–9%	Heat stress	Confusion; impaired vision	Muscle spasms; collapse
9–10%	System on the verge of shutting down	Hallucinations; inability to swallow	Blackouts
+10%	Heat exhaustion	Heat stroke	You could die

Running on empty

In the interests of research for this book, I stopped running for two weeks and went on a very-low-carb diet. I didn't weigh myself, but must have lost a few pounds as my clothes felt looser. Then I went for my regular 10k run around Hampstead Heath. After about five kilometres I could barely lift my feet, and after seven – which had taken me an hour to complete, double the normal time – I was reduced to walking the rest of the route.

Tip: If you are going to use a sports drink during a race, experiment with different brands during training runs to find out which works best and whether your system has an adverse reaction to any of them.

after the first hour you should be alternating water and sports drink (see box below) when you take on fluids.

Finally, don't forget to continue drinking water after the race, as re-hydration will be an important part of your recovery process.

Sports drinks

Sports drinks have been around for just over 50 years, and were invented at a US university as a pretty unappetising solution of salt, sugar and water. It worked though, in that they improved performances by slowing down athletes' rates of dehydration while providing an easily absorbed energy boost. Today, like almost everything else connected with running, sports drinks have been scienced up, but, essentially not much has been changed and they're still a mix of water, carbohydrates and electrolytes.

For a distance runner, the main advantage of sports drinks over plain water is its carbohydrate content: in this form it will get into your system immediately and serve to quickly replenish your

Which sports drink?

There are three types of sports drinks on the market:

Isotonic: The balance of carbs and electrolytes to water is the same as in the human body, so it will be absorbed at around the same speed as water, but has greater calorific value.

Hypotonic: The carbs and electrolyte/water ratio is less that the body's, so the fluid is absorbed quicker than water but with less energy replenishment.

Hypertonic: A greater carbs/electrolyte concentration than the body, so the fluid is absorbed the slowest, but the energy replacement is the greatest. Best as an after-race recovery drink.

How to calculate your fluid needs

Because everybody sweats at a different rate, to get a more precise idea of how quickly you are losing fluid and a far better notion of what you need to replenish it, take this simple test (NB: this has to be worked out in imperial measures because one fluid ounce of water weighs exactly that – one ounce):

1. Weigh yourself naked, in pounds, prior to your run.

2. Keep an accurate account, in fluid ounces of the amount of water you drink during your run.

3. Weigh yourself again as soon as you get back, once more in pounds, also naked and before you have started drinking water. (You weigh yourself naked before and after the run because even the best moisture-control fabric will hold some water.)

4. Subtract the post-run figure from the pre-run figure and multiply by 16 to convert into ounces.

6. Add the figure for water consumed during your run.

7. Divide this figure by the number of hours, or parts of an hour, you have been running.

Because the weight you have lost during your run will be all water and no fat, this will give you a reasonably accurate "sweat rate" for that run. Average this out over a number of runs in similar conditions.

Although this is far from an exact science it will give you a good idea of what sort of quantities you need to drink while running.

Take seasonal averages, because summer running can require twice as much fluid replenishment as during the colder months.

The simple mathematical formula for working out your fluid loss is:

$$\frac{\textbf{(pre-run weight – post run weight) x 16 + fl oz water consumed}}{\textbf{hours run}}$$

(To convert into litres, divide by 20 (16 in the US) and multiply by 0.568)

Here's one we made earlier!

Many runners swear by their own sports drink recipe, and it's not difficult to develop your own combination of sugar, water and salt. Three tablespoons of brown sugar and a generous pinch of salt dissolved in 500ml of water will give you around seven per cent carbs and 0.3 per cent sodium, the equivalent of most isotonic sports drinks – adjust accordingly for hypertonic or hypotonic. The flavouring you add – and you will need flavouring – is up to you, but be aware that adding fresh fruit juice or squash could over-load the carbohydrates because of their intrinsic sugar content.

Fruit squash, diluted to two parts squash/ 10 parts water (isotonic); 1/10 (hypotonic); and 4/10 (hypertonic), with a large pinch of salt, is another popular home-made sports drink for a fraction of the cost. My personal favourite is three parts water to one part cranberry juice, with a big pinch of salt.

Tip: Instead of brown sugar in a home-brewed sports drink, use powdered glucose. Available at any chemist, it will be absorbed into your system quicker. Also, if you're not keen on a salty taste, use sodium citrate instead of table salt as it will give you the same sodium replenishment without tasting like salt.

depleting glycogen stores. Also, the addition of carbohydrate speeds up your body's absorption of the drink's water element. However, for it to be of value to you, a sports drink's carb content has to be between five and eight per cent. If it is much lower, it won't be enough to make any difference and you might as well save your money. If it is higher than eight per cent then the concentration of sugar will actually impede your body's water absorption, will require too much of the energy that should be saved for running to be used up in breaking it down, and will have a hugely increased chance of upsetting your stomach. This is why sugar-rich "energy" drinks are not recommended for runners. Neither is the common practice of drinking sweet fizzy drinks that have been left to go flat – they will have a carb content of twelve per cent or more. Always check the carbohydrate content of a sports drink before buying it.

The other key ingredient is electrolytes, which will be sodium and potassium. There are conflicting schools of thought as to whether the replenishment of these minerals, which you lose through sweating, is advantageous or not, but what has been proved is that a small amount of them in water speeds the hydration process. Electrolytes should be between 0.2 and 0.5 per cent of the drink.

Running gear

Will I need much?
No, you won't.

That's one of the best things about running, nobody needs that much to get started – some shorts, a pair of shoes and you're away. It means that anywhere you travel, you can go for a run, as it won't give you much extra to pack.

Of course, this can work against running as a pastime, as there simply isn't that much clever stuff to buy. Compared with, say, golf, running's gadget count will barely register on even the most impressionable consumer's shopping list.

However, while there might not be much running kit to buy, what there is will be crucial to your performance. And because every runner's needs will be different, getting the wrong gear will be worse than getting no gear at all.

Fact: Less than five per cent of the trainers sold around the world are actually worn to do any form of training. Which probably means that hardly any sneakers do any sneaking either.

Shoes

The single most important piece of kit any runner will own. Choosing them is about much more than brand-name glamour.

Choosing running shoes used to be the easiest thing in the world: they were the same shoes you used to play tennis in or wore for netball or five-a-side football. These days, though, you'll have to pick your way through a jungle of different styles, constructions and technologies, where, just to make matters worse, everything seems to be called "trainers".

Scientific as running shoe design may be, for new runners choosing a pair it is still largely a matter of common sense and trusting your own judgement.

Quite simply you want something that will be comfortable, will protect your feet from the elements and the terrain and will absorb the shock of a fully grown person landing on it several thousand times a week. Label identity or leisure shoe brand preferences shouldn't count for too much, as models and different brands of running shoe will have different characteristics, therefore a brand name you might not have previously considered might be exactly right for your feet. It's worth remembering that, although we all want to look as stylish as possible, as often as possible, there's nothing particularly attractive about hobbling home with your

The best running shoes

There is no "best shoe", only the best shoe for you. And because models and styles change so frequently, it's a issue you'll need to re-address every time you shop for a new pair. Take advice from the shop staff as regards your pronation (see box on p.45), and be willing to try on a few pairs before you find what is your most suitable shoe.

designer shoes in one hand as blood seeps through your socks. A perfect fit is far more important than aesthetic appeal. Whereas you might be able to put up with a less-than-perfect fit on your leisure footwear, after you've covered three or four kilometres on a hot day your running shoes will let you know if they aren't right – in no uncertain terms.

Because everybody's feet are unique, their choice of running shoe should be too. But that doesn't mean you shouldn't talk to experienced runners about their preferences in different conditions. However, make sure you find out why somebody likes or dislikes certain shoes; then you can use that as a starting point in your search. It's always best to talk about particular models rather than brands as a whole, because the ranges are now so wide and are changed so often that it's impossible to pin down any of the top labels to specific characteristics.

Unless you know from past experience exactly what model and size you are going to buy, always shop for your running shoes in either a specialist running shop or a sports store with a dedicated running department. This will greatly increase the chances of the sales staff being runners and not merely shoe salespeople, thus they should have the time and the knowledge to help you make the right choice. Be prepared for a fairly lengthy process as you should have both feet measured and you should be watched running – either in your current shoes or in a pair they select for you. Then both feet of each prospective shoe should be tested out – if it is a small store, go into the street to run a dozen or so paces in them.

You shouldn't be talked into spending too much either. A decent pair of shoes to start off with ought to cost between £50 and £80 (around $120). While you don't want to spend too much before you find out what your needs will be, laying out too little will mean construction has been skimped on and it will be a false economy.

Are you being served?

You'll know you are getting good service in a running shoe shop when you are asked:

How much do you weigh?

How many miles a week do you run?

What distances?

On what terrain do you do most of your running?

How long have you been running?

Do you race?

Have you had any trouble with your feet or shoes?

Is there anything unusual about your stride or strike?

Only after this should you be asked:

How much do you want to spend?

However you approach the task of finding the right running shoes, the effort you put in will be repaid from the moment you hit the road. Just remember the advice in this chapter to get the most out of that time spent shopping for running shoes.

What sort of feet have you got?

Everybody pronates, and as a runner your pronation will be particularly important. It's the degree of roll from the outside of the foot inwards that occurs every time your stride hits the ground. It happens because, for strength and balance in the perfect running stride, the foot naturally lands on its outside edge and rolls inward until the heel lines up directly beneath the calf. At that point it converts all the energy into a forward movement and the alignment of the foot and lower leg stays in this position. But that's the perfect stride, and only about half of all runners have one. The rest of us either overpronate and continue rolling inwards past that optimum point, or supinate which means the foot doesn't roll inwards enough to reach it. Try the Wet Feet Test (see box opposite) to find out what your likely pronation will be.

Incorrect pronation can put dangerous amounts of stress on your knees and ankles, and even affect your lower back

It's very important that your pronation is taken into account when you choose shoes, as the roll performed by your foot as you land is part of a very complex bio-mechanical cushioning procedure taking place to absorb some of the shock of landing. Not compensating for over- or under-pronation will not only affect your performance, as you won't be getting the strongest push from the front of your foot, but can eventually cause discomfort and injury.

There are specific running shoes on the market designed to counteract imbalances in pronation. If you shop in a specialist

The wet feet test

The most reliable way of finding out your foot type is to place a piece of coloured paper, large enough to fit your feet on, on a hard floor (carpet will be too soft to register your footprints) and stand on it in bare feet with wet soles. Your footprints will be close to one of the three illustrations, and from that you can judge what your stride's pronation is likely to be.

High arches: the chances are you will supinate and your stride's natural cushioning capability will be lower than it should be. You will need a cushioned shoe for added shock absorption and it should also have a curved sole to compensate for any dampening of the foot's natural movement brought on by extra cushioning. These shoes are also known as flexibility shoes.

Flat feet: you are probably an overpronator and should be fitted with a motion control shoe – that's one that is much more rigid, with an inflexible heel counter (see box on p.47) and a straight shape. The midsole will be considerably thicker and will contain a bracing medial post to stop the foot rolling inwards. Because of all this added support these will be the heaviest running shoes.

Normal feet: you have a normal pronation which calls for normal shoes, so you shouldn't have to look for any special properties. Ideally you need one with a semi-curved sole and as much cushioning as you feel comfortable with.

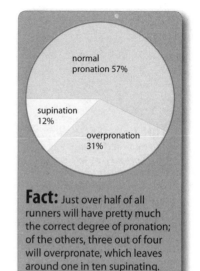

normal pronation 57%

supination 12%

overpronation 31%

Fact: Just over half of all runners will have pretty much the correct degree of pronation; of the others, three out of four will overpronate, which leaves around one in ten supinating.

running shop, the first thing they should do is ask to see you run. Only then will they pronounce on your pronation and be able to fit you with the correct shoes.

Different shoes for different runs

Not all running surfaces and conditions are the same, so there are different shoe types to allow you to get the best out of whatever kind of running you do most often. The four most common are:

Road shoes

Most of the running shoes on the market are road shoes. They will be relatively heavy as they are well cushioned to provide the most comfort as you pound the pavement, and the soles will be very hardwearing. The outsole (see box opposite) will be curved upwards slightly at the toes to propel you forward but flat enough to ensure stability.

Ideal for: beginners and non-competitive runners.

Performance training shoes

A lighter version of the above, with much of the cushioning removed and a steeper curve to the last for added responsiveness. They will also have made sacrifices as regards stabilizing materials, thus are not recommended for runners who over-pronate or supinate.

Ideal for: fast runners, or racers who need greater stability than is offered by race shoes.

Race shoes

Ultra-lightweight shoes, with a fully curved last and virtually all cushioning and stability materials removed in the quest to strip away apparently excess grams.

Ideal for: elite runners, sub-three-hour marathoners.

Tip: If you can't find different width fittings for the shoes you are looking at, compare different models by holding them upside down next to each other, then select which seems most suitable for you. You'll be surprised at how much they can vary.

When buying running shoes, go for stability over light weight. It's always a trade off, and while you don't want great big clodhoppers, the main function of shoes is to prevent injury by absorbing impact, and you will run far more confidently if you feel well supported.
Hugh Jones

Trail shoes

With heavier, ruggedly constructed uppers and outer elements, these shoes have greater grips on their soles to cope with off-road surfaces. Because terrain will often be softer, they will have less cushioning than road shoes to compensate for reduced responsiveness.

Ideal for: cross-country runners.

What makes shoes run?

Starting from the bottom, a running shoe's outsole – the bit that hits the road – will be made of rugged carbon rubber, or aerated blown rubber. The former is more durable, the latter provides better cushioning. Midsoles are on top of that and are the most important component as that's where the flexibility/rigidity balances are made. The basic midsole material will be EVA or polyurethane, although modern shoes' cushioning is adjusted with internal pockets of gel, liquid or air, or various "energy return" devices. Insoles are largely for comfort and serious runners will prolong the life of shoes by replacing the manufacturers' insoles with specialist versions. The heel counter is a rigid piece of support, designed to hold your heel upright and prevent lateral movement. Uppers are usually of synthetic material, made for lightness and strength and often in a weave that allows air to pass through.

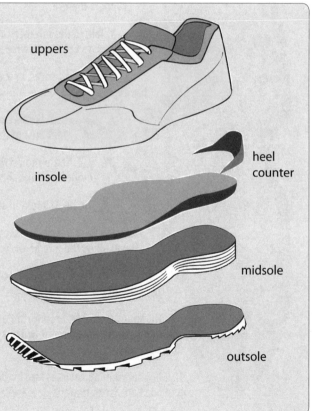

uppers

insole

heel counter

midsole

outsole

10 tips for buying running shoes

1. Go to a specialist running shop – the chances are the sales force will be runners themselves.

2. Talk to the salesperson about what you want – if they haven't got time to talk to you properly they don't deserve your business.

3. Wear athletic socks, or if you haven't got any with you the store should have some for you to use. And if you don't own any, buy some!

4. Make sure both feet are measured, as most people's feet are not the same size.

5. There should be about 10mm between the end of your longest toe and the end of the shoe. Press down to find out.

6. The heel should fit snugly without any movement up and down.

7. Let the sales person see you run before you start choosing shoes; it will allow them to assess your pronation.

8. Have a run in all prospective choices before you make your selection – the shop should encourage this.

9. The shoes should feel comfortable – supporting and cushioning, not pinching – from the moment you put them on. Running shoes should not need to be broken in.

10. Shop for running shoes as late in the day as possible, as your feet can expand up to one half size during the day, and will do the same on a long run.

Take care of your shoes

Look after your shoes and they'll look after you, a maxim every runner should remember. A well-kept pair of shoes will provide much more comfort and support for a longer amount of time than a neglected pair. Although most modern running shoes are made of durable, impervious fabric and need very little care, if you follow these dos and don'ts, you will get the maximum mileage out of them.

✗ Don't put your shoes through the washing machine unless you absolutely have to, as it is far too intense an experience to do them any good.

✔ Wash with mild detergent and lukewarm water.

✔ Wash or clean as soon as possible after your run.

✔ Dry by filling with scrunched up newspaper and leaving in an airy space, after you have removed the insoles.

✗ Don't use your running shoes for any other sport – especially not football.

✔ Remove dried-on mud with a suede brush or a soft dry scrubbing brush.

✗ Don't leave them to dry on a radiator, as they will dry too quickly and the intense heat will damage the midsole.

✔ Store away from bright sunlight and out of any extreme cold. Don't leave them on the porch or in the garden all year round.

✔ Have more than one pair. Each will last longer than they would by themselves as you will have more chance to care for them properly in between runs.

Tip: Stick with what you know. If you are satisfied with a particular model buy it again. And again. If you see it on sale, buy more than one pair, as it seems that companies make it their business to discontinue a shoe just as you've grown to love it.

running gear

Lace meeting

That apparently superfluous perforation at the top of a good running shoe's line of lace holes serves a very real purpose. It allows you to pull the uppers closer around the top of your foot, so keeping your heel snug in the back of the shoe. To make use of it follow the picture below:

1. Lace the shoes crisscross fashion from the toes up.

2. Bring the lace up through the bottom of the regular top hole then down into that extra hole to form a loop. Do this on both sides.

3. Bring the laces across and through their opposite loops.

4. Bring them back together in the centre and tie with a double bow.

NB: The loops created should be about a centimetre long and not pull toward the centre of the tongue.

Know when to say goodbye

Running shoes don't last for ever – if you're covering 30 miles a week, you'll be lucky to get six months out of a pair. Most modern running shoes aren't built to last much more than 500 miles – more if you don't weigh a great deal, less if you're heavier than average. And this is regardless of price, although the very expensive shoes will probably have sturdier uppers and inner fabric.

Shoes can also be knackered and show no signs of wear because the midsole gets destroyed from the constant pounding it's been taking. It collapses, losing any cushioning, meaning that every strike is coming down unprotected. Heel counters will loose their stability around the same time and no longer hold your heel straight. Then, once the inners go, essential flexibility is lost, meaning uppers will tear or tear away from the soles, and the fabric inside will get worn as your feet start rubbing. This will quickly cause blisters, but if shoes have no effective midsole, shins, calves, knees and ankles suffer terrible jolting meaning serious injury is never far away.

Once a shoe wears to this point it will throw you off your usual running stride. Not only will it no longer compensate for any pronation problems you might have, it will also cause you to run in a way that is neither your best or best for you.

Tip: Write the date you started using a pair of shoes somewhere on them – pick a place where it won't rub away. If you know how much mileage you are doing each week it will help you judge when to replace them.

Your shoes are on their uppers if...

On a level surface, either of the backs doesn't point straight up – the heel support is gone.

You can remove the insole then press into the midsole and the dent you've made doesn't spring back immediately – the shoe has lost its cushioning.

The outside of the midsole looks wrinkled – the inside of it has got compressed.

There is a newly noticeable consistent rubbing inside or new tears on the uppers – they will have lost their flexibility.

Your knees and ankles are hurting after relatively easy runs – the midsoles have collapsed.

Shorts 'n' shirts 'n' stuff

There's been as much science applied to running clothing over the last ten years as there has to running shoes. And nearly all of it has been specifically for your comfort.

If most people burrow far enough into their wardrobes, they'll be able to emerge with an ancient pair of gym shorts and the sort of dodgy old t-shirt that was last worn to clear out the guttering. And, provided they've got the right shoes, they've got all they need to go running. Well, everybody's got socks, haven't they?

What they won't have, though, is all they need to run particularly well.

The kind of clothes Oxfam would think twice about are fine if you want to go for a couple of laps around the local park to see if you like it or not, but once you've decided to take running seriously, you're going need some serious kit. Although the even the most exciting technological developments in running clothing won't shave too many minutes off most runners' times, they will make their runs feel much more comfortable.

Shorts

Apart from shoes, a runner's only vital piece of equipment is a pair of shorts. And, second to shoes, they are the most important piece of kit to get right.

Shorts come in various styles and materials, with different shapes for men and women. You should expect to pay around £25 ($40). There are unisex running shorts on the market, but they won't cost much less and will never be as comfortable as gender-specific styles. All good running shorts will have an in-built liner made of soft, lightweight wicking material: in men's shorts this should provide enough support so that you don't need to wear anything underneath, but women will still need underwear (see box on p.54).

The main stylistic differences are leg length and outer seam construction. Length is measured along the inseam, varying between 2.5cm and 18cm as shorts designed specifically for running will always be short so as not to impede movement. Different constructions have different splits in the outseam. This can range from a v-shaped cut of around 3cm at the hem, through half- and three-quarters splits, to a seam that is not sewn at all – the front panel fabric is set on top of the rear in a deeply overlapping layer. The longer splits usually go with the shorter leg lengths for the greatest freedom of movement, therefore sprinters would be advised to go for the shorter, least restrictive cuts. This is, however, far less crucial for distance running.

What you chose in the beginning should be dictated by what is most suitable for your body shape and whatever you feel most comfortable in. That's "comfortable" as in not embarrassed as well as not chafing, because much of the initial resistance to going running is due to self-consciousness about getting out on the streets in athletic gear.

As regards material, today's technology has created fabrics that are light, allow air to flow through to the body, wick sweat away from the skin and dry out quickly (see box on p.55). All the major sportswear companies have their own brand-name performance fabrics, and although most are pretty much the same, it's still best to check on the label that whatever you are buying has the properties you need. These high-tech fabrics are the only thing you should consider; nylon should be avoided as it can rub brutally, and cotton t-shirt or sweatshirt material isn't a good idea for long runs or hot days, as the shorts will absorb sweat and get heavy, then start to sag and flap uncomfortably.

Tip: Take as little as possible with you when you go for a run – I tape my house keys and (in case I have to make an emergency phone call) two 20p pieces to my ankle under my sock and leave it at that. This will solve any pocket-related problems, and, importantly, "de-junking" your run helps you mentally escape everyday life for an hour or two, allowing the greatest spiritual benefit.

Side pockets are, essentially, a distraction to runners, as you'll probably be tempted to put stuff in them – keys, loose change, mobile phone, etc – and whatever it is will bang about against your thighs until it drives you bonkers.

If you have to take stuff with you when you run, you'd be better served keeping your keys and so on in a wrist or ankle pouch, or, if there's *that* much, then you've probably still got a bum bag lurking somewhere in your house.

Most high-performance running shorts have a small key pocket at the waistband, and increasingly they are being designed with dedicated stable enclosures for phones or mp3 players. These are not necessarily such a good idea – see box left.

What to underwear

Although most men's running shorts will have a built-in liner, many don't, and women's shorts will require underwear. The rules are straightforward and more or less the same as for the shorts themselves: stay away from cotton as it absorbs moisture and go for something that is comfortable, won't ride up anywhere and provides enough support. For these reasons, it is not a good idea for men to go running wearing boxer shorts, and women are much better off in Bridget Jones-style big knickers than thongs.

Shirts

Whether you opt to run in a singlet or a short- or long-sleeved shirt is a matter of individual preference, and, as per your choice of shorts, based largely on comfort and modesty. The most important aspect of a running top is what it's made of, and there is really only one rule: don't wear cotton.

What is wicking?

All the major sportswear manufacturers have developed their own wicking fabrics – Dri-fit, Clima Lite, Cool Max, and so on – and in spite of copyright differences, they will all perform much the same function in much the same manner. By taking a three-dimensional approach to fabric construction, they use the depth of the material to actively channel sweat away from the skin to the garment's outer surface, where it will quickly evaporate, and not gather in the material or flow back towards the body.

Where the fabric makes contact with the skin it will have a more open surface area, achieved by the bigger gaps between the fibres' internal strands, which allow it to soak up sweat more efficiently. The polyester (or similar) construction material will not absorb the sweat, but the size and direction of the weave will push it outwards towards the material's external side. As it travels, the sweat condenses from water vapour to liquid and cannot reverse its direction because the weave is big enough to allow vapour through but too small to accommodate liquid, which is why these fabrics can let sweat out but not allow rain in.

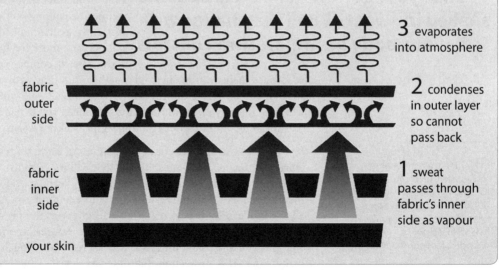

3 evaporates into atmosphere

fabric outer side

2 condenses in outer layer so cannot pass back

fabric inner side

1 sweat passes through fabric's inner side as vapour

your skin

I advised against running in cotton gym shorts in the previous section, and those effects will be far more acute when it comes to shirts. However, the temptation to run in a cotton t-shirt will at first be enormous: everybody's got a few; they're comfortable; that's surely what they were designed for in the first place; and when those grey shirts show up how much you're sweating you look like a proper athlete, which has to be cool... But this is wrong on nearly every level, especially the last.

All your problems start with sweat, and the way that grey t-shirt will show it up is a vivid illustration: the garment's fibres are absorbing your sweat instead of removing it from your skin and speeding evaporation. Once the t-shirt has become soaked in sweat, quite apart from being heavy, uncomfortable and abrasive, it will play havoc with your body's temperature controls. In hot weather, as the sweat will not be moving away from your skin properly it will not be cooling you down as efficiently as it might, thus you will perspire more freely as your body tries to compensate. This will speed dehydration. In cold weather, running with a sweat-soaked wet shirt and the resulting wet skin will chill your body, which is not only uncomfortable but will mean you expend energy that could be put into your running simply to keep warm.

> **Once your cotton t-shirt has become soaked in sweat, it will play havoc with your body's temperature controls**

You will run much more comfortably in a top made from artificial fabric that has wicking capability as that will move moisture away from your skin and hasten its evaporation, keeping you dry and therefore cool or warm in response to your environment. Although all the modern high-tech materials will give you the perspiration control cotton can't, there will also be extra features on offer. Most will give you a brushed inner surface to create soft "touch points", many offer UV protection (at differing levels), and the more

Tip: Men: when running on a beach, take your shirt off and run bare-chested. It'll make you feel like some sort of warrior and if you're trying to lose weight will do wonders for your motivation.

advanced tops feature climate control that will open or close the weave to adjust air permeability in reaction to the temperature. Check the properties on the label to make sure a shirt will do what you want. Depending on its features, a running top will cost you between £25 and £50 (between $40 and $70).

Sports bras

According to the lingerie industry, roughly seventy per cent of the UK's women are wearing bras that don't fit properly, and it doesn't seem to worry them too much. Sports bras, however, are a different matter. They will be chosen solely for function, and as they have to work hard they'll become unbearable if they don't fit properly.

First determine your fit, then decide what type of sports bra you need. As you try them on, road test them in the shop by running fairly vigorously on the spot – this will give more vertical movement than will usually occur on your runs and so will be a good test. To check your size, measure around your rib cage, underneath your breasts, and add five inches to the figure. This is your band size. Then measure around your breasts at the widest point. Compare the two numbers and consult the chart below to find your cup size. For example, if the second figure is two inches bigger than the first you should try a B cup, if it is three inches bigger a C cup, and so on.

Up to 1 inch larger	A cup
Between 1 and 2 inches	B cup
Between 2 and 3 inches	C cup
Between 3 and 4 inches	D cup
Between 4 and 6 inches	DD or E cup
6 inches larger	F cup

Fact: The first sports bra was created in 1977 by Americans Hindra Miller and Lisa Lindahl when they sewed two jockstraps together. They formed the Jogbra company and within 10 years were multi-millionaires. An original Jogbra is currently in New York's Metropolitan Museum of Art.

Fact: A good sports bra will survive about 50 machine washes before it starts to lose its grip. Hand washing will prolong its life, but on no account put it in the drier as that will break down the moisture wicking capability and destroy its elasticity.

Tip: Because encapsulation bras separate the breasts, they are often preferred as they eliminate the "uniboob" look that can result from compression styles.

Six things to look for when choosing a sports bra:

No seams or no internal seams

Wide shoulder straps (between 10 and 20mm)

Soft all over

Made from moisture wicking, breathable fabric

No fastenings (pullover style) or padding around the hooks to prevent them chafing

Wide stretch band around rib cage to prevent the bra from riding up

Tip: For an animated interactive test to help you find the right sports bra, visit **www.shockabsorber.co.uk**

// A good sports bra is an absolute must, and it has to fit properly. Don't be fobbed off! If you want to run properly for any length of time there has to be very little movement going on up there. //
Efua Baker

The type of sports bra that would be best for you depends on the activity involved and what size you are. Running is a high-impact activity and your breasts will need much more motion control than for, say, tennis (medium impact), so the most suitable bra types will be compression or encapsulation.

A compression bra pretty much does what it says on the tin and will control your breasts by pressing them into your chest. This is likely to be a pullover design rather than one with fastenings. Compression bras are not recommended for runners over a B cup, as they cannot firmly control larger breasts, Also, the larger the cup size, the more awkward it will be to put on.

Encapsulation bras are not dissimilar to the original double jockstrap sports bra prototype (see box on p.57) and are much more suitable for large cup sizes, as they hold each breast separately and control motion in the cup rather than against the body. These models are much more likely to have fastenings, so make sure they are covered and cannot chafe against your skin.

Socks

It's remarkable how so many runners put so much time and expense into finding the right shoes, only to wear them with totally unsuitable socks or, worse still, no socks at all. To prevent even the best-fitting running shoes chafing, you will have to wear socks, and socks that come up above the backs of the shoes so that they won't slip down easily and cause discomfort.

Once again, avoid cotton and opt for specialized running socks of a synthetic material that will move sweat away from your feet. There will be a range of cushioning on offer and what you end up with will be a matter of personal preference, best decided after trying out several different types.

Once you have selected your sock type, don't continue with them after they have started to wear thin as they will no longer be functioning. And always make sure you have a pair with you when you go to buy shoes.

Winter warming

In colder conditions the secret to staying warm but not overheating has always been layering, but during the last decade or so, thanks to modern, high-performance fabrics, it has become much easier. Gone are the days when wintry conditions meant bulky sweat suits, fleeces or quilted anoraks. Your winter wardrobe should comprise a base garment, a running suit or a pair of tights and a running jacket, a long-sleeved shirt, a close-fitting soft hat and a pair of gloves. The idea is that garments are removed or replaced as the climate and your body temperature varies.

Let's start closest to the skin with the base layer. Its primary purpose is to wick sweat from your body, and will be a thin, light, tight-fitting top, preferably seamless and longer than a standard running top to make sure it remains tucked in. In really cold conditions a middle layer of a long-sleeved running shirt can also be worn. Over that will be the outer layer of a running jacket made from breathable, windproof and waterproof material.

Jackets are available as basic "hard shell", a single-layer, weatherproof construction, or as "soft shell", containing a soft lining for warmth, which would take the place of a mid-layer. While the latter will be less bulky than two layers, you will lose the option to peel off gradually. Any running jacket you buy should have front and rear reflective strips, as the chances of running after dark are much greater in the winter. Expect to pay around £20 ($35) for a base layer, £40 ($70) for a hard-shell jacket and up to £70 ($120) for a soft-shell.

Tip: Don't overdress, because once you start running you'll heat up very quickly. A most common cold-weather mistake is starting a run with too many clothes on. You should be dressed lightly enough to notice the cold with a degree of discomfort as you walk out of your front door, but not so as to make it unbearable.

Tip: If you can find one, buy a running jacket with detachable sleeves. It will be well worth the extra you will pay as zipping the sleeves off once you've warmed up will prevent you overheating, but you will really feel the benefit of a windproof covering across your chest.

Tights, or leggings, perform a double function: protect you from a cold wind and, if they have a decent stretch fabric content, will give you some compression and so help you warm up more quickly (see p.61). Running tights will be ergonomically contoured – men's and women's tights are different – so they won't interfere with your stride, and to get maximum benefit they should be windproof, water resistant and breathable and have wicking properties. The degree of warmth on offer will vary from artic-proof to lighter models more suited to mild city winters, and they should cost between £30 and £60 ($50 to $100), depending on their capacity.

Running suits are an increasingly popular alternative to tights and a jacket, and are, essentially, a highly evolved version of the old 1980s shell suits. They're very similar to the soft-shell jacket described previously, but come with matching trousers, and will be water resistant, windproof and breathable. They should be worn over a base layer and shorts or support briefs, and models will be available to cope with varying extremes of winter. The advantages of a running suit over tights and a jacket is the option to wear shorts underneath the trousers and thus "layer off" below as well as above the waist. But they will be loose-fitting, thus bulkier than tights, lacking any compression and with the potential to flap around.

Should you go for a running suit or tights and a jacket? It's a debate that starts up everywhere runners gather in less-than-temperate conditions and, like the choice of running shirts, is strictly a matter of whatever you feel most comfortable wearing. You shouldn't pay more than £120 ($200) for a good running suit.

Hats and gloves

It's not unusual to see a runner out on a frosty morning wearing a singlet and the most minimal split shorts, but a fleece hat and gloves as well. In fact it could even be me. While this might seem

The cost of running:	
Shoes	£70 ($120)
Shorts	£25 ($40)
Shirts x 2	£45 ($75)
Jacket	£35 ($50)
Tights	£30 ($45)
Hat and gloves	£12 ($20)
Socks x 3	£7 ($12)
Sports bra*	£20 ($35)
Watch/heart-rate monitor	£70 ($120)
TOTAL	£314 ($517)

* Not required by most male runners

paradoxical there are very good reasons to wrap up the head and hands when everything else is exposed to the elements. You lose about 40 per cent of your body heat through your head, so keeping that covered will stop you freezing over before you've warmed up. Plus, in very cold conditions your body will divert blood away from your extremities to service vital organs, thus your hands can get disproportionately cold – as can your feet, especially in open weave running shoes. There are plenty of specialist, moisture-managing "athletic" hats and gloves in the shops, and they probably work splendidly, but any wool or fleece garments will do it just as well and probably won't cost nearly as much.

Don't forget about covering your head in the summer too, especially if the thatch isn't quite as luxuriant as it used to be – you could be out in the sun for three or four hours, meaning sunburn or sunstroke is a very real possibility. As you'd expect, there are brand-name summer running caps on the market, but the baseball cap remains the most popular option, to be turned back to front *only* if there are wind issues or you are under 10 years old.

Compression shorts

These are far from being basic kit, and will not be needed by most runners – I have run for 25 years and have never gone near a pair yet. However, other runners I know wouldn't leave home without them. They do have certain benefits, but as they aren't cheap, they should be chosen carefully.

Tight-fitting, trunks-style garments, they are worn under running shorts and go from waist to mid-thigh or just above the knee. You should go for compression shorts designed specifically for running, and they will be shaped appropriately for men and women. As the name suggests, they will be made of an expandable material – usually involving a percentage of Lycra or Spandex.

They work by compressing the muscles, and their construction means they separate the hamstring and groin muscles, providing strong support and preventing any chafing that would ultimately irritate the sciatic nerve. By squeezing the waist and thighs they constrict blood vessels to generate and maintain heat within the muscles, thus allowing them to warm up faster and become less susceptible to early strains.

Many runners swear that compression shorts improve their performance, as by holding the muscles tight they prevent energy loss through oscillations – lateral movement of the muscle's fibres. It is also claimed that keeping the muscles moving in one direction increases momentum. Although there is little scientific evidence of this, just thinking it's happening might provide enough of a psychological lift to give a faster time.

Pricier compression shorts have removable washable linings, otherwise you'll need underwear. Expect to pay between £30 and £40 (between $50 and $70) for a good pair, and choose them based on how much resistance they put up to expansion.

Gadgets

As a runner, there aren't really that many gadgets for you to buy, and even less that will make any real difference to your ability or comfort, but here is a run down of the really useful ones.

Watches

No matter how laid back and non-competitive you think you are about your running, at some point you will want to know if you are getting any better, or what time you could actually do a 10k race in.

And you'll want to be able to time yourself with a greater degree of accuracy than "When I went out, the kitchen clock said about twenty past". You need a runner's watch, and it needs to have certain basic functions. Although, depending on how much you want to pay, there seems to be no limit to the number of functions a sports watch can perform, there are four that are a must.

First, it should tell the time – not the time of your run but the time of day. You will need to know it, and on many of your runs there won't be that many people around to ask. Second, it needs to be a stopwatch, timing from hours down to tenths of a second, and preferably more sophisticated than a simple start/stop. You should be able to stop it to check on lap times or times at mile markers while it still carries on timing the run as a whole, and it should be able to record each of your runs in sections so that when you are running splits you can see what speed you have been doing during different stages.

Third, the watch should have a memory so you can display and sort through previous run/lap times to compare them with what you are doing that day – many will automatically locate personal bests. It's worth looking for a watch with a dual display mode that will allow you to view a previous run's timing when you are out on another one. A watch's memory can also provide an easily accessible training log, and some of the more sophisticated models will allow you to download the memory to your computer.

The final must-have feature is a countdown timer with a beeping facility. This is great if you are running splits or doing Fartlek anywhere other than a track, as it can be set to sound when you need to switch intensity. It can also work the other way and beep at whatever interval you want to be doing a set distance in, allowing you to adjust your pace. Or it can simply provide an ongoing record of a time you're trying to beat, and, if you have dual display, you will be able to continually compare it with what time you are doing.

Heart-rate monitors

To train smarter as well as harder, you really need a heart-rate monitor. This is a two-part piece of kit consisting of a belt that goes around your chest registering your heartbeat, and a receiver with a digital read-out on your wrist that receives the transmissions of your heartbeat. The most basic models (costing around £30 or $50) will do simply that, providing a constant monitor, which will allow you to push yourself harder or to slow down as you strive to get the most, in terms of a workout, out of your run.

At the next level up (costing around £40–£60 or $75–$110), as well as the continuous read-out, the monitors can be programmed to sound audible warnings at upper and lower heart rates, to beep at different levels relating to different targets of aerobic intensity, and to tell you when you have warmed up and how your cooling down is progressing. Heart-rate monitors are available with memories to allow you to review sessions at your convenience (expect to pay at least £100 for these models), and, like sports watches, the top-of-the-range monitors come with cabling and software to download a run's information to your computer where you'll be able to chart and analyse the results in much greater depth. These will set you back anything from £150 to £350 ($250 to $600).

Fact: Most decent heart-rate monitors will incorporate basic sports watch functions, so don't forget this aspect if shopping for both devices.

Running buggies

When you consider the cost of childcare, between £300 and £500 ($500 to $1200) for a hard-wearing, smooth-rolling running buggy doesn't seem quite so extortionate. Even less so when you factor in the benefits: you're getting back to exercising; you're enjoying some fresh air together; your baby's absorbent mind is being exposed to all sorts of interesting scenery; and you both stand a good chance of meeting like-minded souls.

In the last few years, the demand for running buggies has been enormous, which means there is now a bewildering amount of choice. Beyond the features you'd expect on an everyday buggy – efficient braking, straightforward collapsibility, weather protection, infant comfort, washable linings, etc – when choosing running buggy you should look for the following:

Larger wheels
This reduces the amount they need to turn, meaning a smoother ride for baby and less pushing for you. Standard sizes are 12 inches in diameter, for gentle jogging on smooth surfaces; 16 inches for running on pavements, cinder tracks and even fields with short grass; and 20 inches and above, for competitive and long distance running or off-road use.

Alloy wheels

These are more expensive than steel but much lighter, therefore pushing the buggy won't sap so much of your strength. Also, they are much easier to clean and will not rust after you've been out in the rain or across muddy ground.

Fixed front wheel

It shouldn't swivel for steering because it is this that will give you the firm tracking and stability you need for confident running. Unfortunately this means it won't be particularly manoeuvrable in everyday situations like a crowded high street. There are running buggies on the market with a front wheel that can be locked straight or allowed to swivel, but these might not be such a good buy for the serious runner; they seldom have wheels over 12 inches in diameter and the front-wheel joint won't be strong enough to take a lot of running on surfaces other than those that are flat and even.

Pneumatic tyres

These will require a bit of maintenance and may get the occasional puncture but will make pushing across uneven ground mush easier and will give baby a smoother ride – don't forget there's nothing like an unhappy infant to cut short a run.

Adjustable handlebar

Because not everybody is the same height, obviously, and when you go running you will need to set your buggy up in a way that allows you to run as naturally and efficiently as possible. Which might not be the same position you require when strolling with it.

Tough but yielding construction

Look for a welded aluminium frame, as this will be both light and strong enough to withstand the rigours of off-roading. The frame should also have built-in shock absorbers to give your passenger the most untroubled ride.

Five-point safety harness

If baby is strapped in as securely as possible not only will they settle easier, but you will feel much more confident and therefore much more relaxed, about running faster.

Backpacks

If you're considering regularly running to work, college or anywhere where you're going to need to change clothes on arrival, then a runner's backpack will be vital. Prices start at about three times the cost of a decent everyday backpack – from around £60 up to a couple of hundred ($100 to $400) – but the difference between a specialist item and an ordinary model will be noticeable within just a few hundred yards.

It should be a given that a runner's backpack will be light, rugged and weatherproof, but it should also be ergonomically shaped, with cutaways at the sides so as not to interfere with arm movement. As a runner you will have a much greater need for load stability, and a good backpack will have plenty of compartments and pockets inside to keep contents from shifting about. To stop the whole thing bouncing, the shoulder straps will be supplemented with a strap going across the chest or sternum, while many models also feature a detachable hip strap. All straps will be finely adjustable and made from breathable, cushioned material.

Tip: Because good runners' backpacks are light and strong and have a greater emphasis on ergonomics and weight distribution than regular rucksacks, despite the extra expense they can also represent a better buy for everyday use.

Tip: There are a number of runners' belts on the market. Balanced and snug fitting, they feature water bottle holders or bladders and stable compartments for items such as keys, change and sunglasses. They are a useful alternative if you don't need to carry too much.

Any part of the pack in continual contact with your shirt will be made from a wicking fabric to prevent sweat collecting underneath it – the more advanced models are constructed to allow air to pass between the back and the surface of the pack. There should be a couple of pockets that can be reached without taking it off. Likewise any water bottle holders need to be easily accessible, and loops or rings should be attached to zips to make them much easier to locate while on the move.

As you move up the price spectrum, runners' backpacks become increasingly specialized. Many models, often referred to as "camelbacks", feature built-in bladders to allow you to drink via a tube while running. There are also some featuring rigid, padded compartments for laptops, and certain larger models even claim to carry a business suit without crushing it. Of course, with these last two options will come a considerable increase in weight.

Sunglasses

Because so much running is done in evenings or early mornings when the sun is low in the sky, sunglasses have long been a popular runners' accessory. During the last decade or so, as sportswear has become more scientific, equipment manufacturers and optical companies have devoted increasing resources to developing sports-friendly sunglasses. With ranges made from materials that weren't even invented ten years ago, with "image intensifying capability" and even with built-in mp3 players, there's a great deal on offer. As you'll be expected to spend between £35 and £200 (£50 to $350), there's much you should know in order to make the best buy.

Weight and durability of both frames and lenses will be of prime concern, and different manufacturers will use their patented materials – simply look for impact-resistance guarantees and scratch

Fact: The most efficient colour for sunglasses lenses is grey, as it will decrease the level of light being allowed through without affecting colours. Except for making them a bit darker, obviously.

proofing, and test for flexibility when buying. You shouldn't consider sunglasses that block less than 99 per cent of UVA and UVB rays – UVB is the type proven to damage the eyes, and although there is little evidence of UVA harm, medical debate currently rages about potential danger. This aspect is vital, so look for manufacturers' specifications rather than store recommendations.

Glasses should filter out about 80 per cent of visible light. A handy test when choosing non-light-reactive sunglasses is to try them on three or four feet from the shop's mirror – if you can see your eyes clearly they will not filter out enough light when you're out running. There are several sports sunglasses "systems" on the market now that allow you to change lenses for bright or dimmer light, or even use clear lenses for the physical eye protection factor alone. Polarizing or mirror-coated lenses are best if you are expecting to experience intense glare, and if you opt for photochromatic (light-sensitive) lenses, make sure they are at the faster-reacting end of the scale.

Fit is hugely important for a runner as nothing will be more irritating than glasses that bounce on your face as you stride. A sleek, aerodynamic shape will cut down on movement caused by air flow as you run, as well as making you look fairly hardcore, but non-slip grips on the side arms and nose pads are recommended to combat your inevitable sweat. The top-of-the-range models will have variable fitting with adjustable side arms and interchangeable nose pads.

mp3 players

There are two conflicting schools of thought regarding mp3 players and running: those who find the motivational qualities of particular popular songs vital to get the most out of their running experience, and those who appreciate the clear headspace that running brings

Fact: Wraparound sun-glasses provide much better UV protection as they will filter out rays coming from the sides.

Tip: To check there are no imperfections on the lenses of sunglasses, before you buy hold them at arm's length, look through one lens at a straight line – a shelf or a door – and move the lens across it. Turn the lens sideways and repeat, then do the same with the other lens. In every case the line should stay straight. If it distorts, the lens is not true.

If you always run with an iPod, try running without every so often, just to change your experience. Similarly, if you always run in a group, try it by yourself. It's very important that you don't become dependent on any one single set of conditions.
Karen Hancock

Tip: If you have trouble deciding what music to listen to on the move, check out *The Rough Guide Book Of Playlists* (£7.99) which contains more than 500 expertly compiled soundtracks ranging from kraut rock to Curtis Mayfield by way of songs about cats and dogs.

and/or the sounds that surround them. But these days, with *RunCity*'s city runs guided and commentated on mp3, and an increasing number of ebooks available, there's much more to it than just getting that perfect running beat.

Of course there are always going to be safety issues if you entirely block out your environment while out on the streets (see pp.136–143), so those big noise-cancelling headphones that are just right for the train aren't really the smartest thing to run with. Nor are the very expensive brand-name mp3 players.

Whatever soundtrack you play while you're running, you should be listening to it on the smallest, cheapest mp3 player your can bear to be seen with. For no other reason than Sod's Law: the odds of you dropping it, falling over on it, steaming it up with condensation or getting it soaked in the rain will be considerably shortened if you opt to cruise round the park carrying a £300 ($500) hard drive. You'll be of far more interest to the local hoodies, too.

Tip: Don't ever go running with irreplaceable songs on your mp3 player. That is when you're sure to suffer a mishap – make sure all those rare grooves are copied on to the one you leave at home.

The shrewder music-loving runner invests £20 ($30) or so in a small-capacity, no-name brand model and leaves the video-capable 10,000-song unit safely indoors. You'll seldom need more than fifty or sixty tunes for a run and the quality of bass reproduction won't be such an issue as you hit the wall. These thing are about the same size and weight as a throwaway lighter. In fact, it's probably best to assume this inexpensive mp3 player is throwaway, then you won't feel too upset if something does happen to it on the road.

GPS devices

These are costly (upwards of £200/$400), bulky (hand-held devices weigh between 15 and 20g), or virtually unreadable (the wrist models have tiny screens), and probably not necessary for anybody other than the most ardent gadget freak. The simple truth is most runners do the same runs over and over again, and rely on friends or mild exploration to find a new route. They rarely get lost or put themselves in a position where they could get lost. Even for running in a foreign city, there are guides such as those by *RunCity* or *Runner's World* that detail interesting routes in an easy-to-follow fashion. GPS monitors can be useful to track exactly what distances you have travelled during a run, but there are plenty of easily accessible websites that will accurately measure your mileage in the comfort of your own home, provided you can remember the route.

Technology in action

There was a time when running was considered a pure sport, just you against yourself and the elements, with nothing added to your muscle power other than a decent pair of shoes. Not any more. Although running remains essentially a matter of human achievement – aside from shoes and clothing fabric there aren't a great many advantages to be bought – personal technology is becoming so commonplace that at some events the beeping of digital devices threatens to drown out the pounding of feet.

Tip: GPS devices are much better suited to cyclists as they will travel much further much faster.

A heart-rate monitor is about the only really worthwhile gadget. It certainly helps new runners control themselves, keeping them out of oxygen deficit and stopping them going off too quick. You can train far more specifically with one. Not sure of the value of a GPS device though. **Hugh Jones**

Timing chips

Big races have been providing timing chips for entrants to attach to their shoes for years. These activate a signal as the runner passes over a mat at the start and the finish and maybe a couple of points in between, and are programmed with the runner's number, thus giving a precise timing for the run that will be posted on the race website. Recently, though, telecom companies have expanded this technology to access the internet directly and, operating in real time, provide a remote tracking service for access by both racers and their supporters.

A runner buys a chip not unlike the one described above, that will register as he passes wireless hotspots at various distances around the course, sending an online signal to that runner's designated "page" on a website set up by the chip supplier. Friends and family will be able to follow their progress in the race from anywhere in the world. The chips will also send text messages or emails alerts as each point is passed, and in areas that are totally covered by a wireless network, progress can be continuously monitored. Most of these services provide live streaming from the finish too, so virtual spectators can watch their tracked racers cross the line. Virtually.

The other popular use of systems such as this is to receive signals to your mobile phone, allowing you to monitor your own progress and timing splits and pace yourself. As these services will also send a detailed breakdown of your race to your computer, performance analysis will be much easier and you will have a set of tangible figures upon which to build your next training schedule.

Interactive clothing

Interactive clothing is increasing in popularity too. There are several sports bras on the market with built-in heart-rate monitors that read out, wirelessly, to a screen on your wrist. Sportswear giant Adidas has joined forces with Polar, who make digital heart-rate monitors and athletes' chronometers, to produce a range of running tops incorporating heart-rate monitors and running shoes with accelerometers in the sole. These are digital gizmos that, once calibrated to the wearer's stride length and using the forces of inertia and space-age gyroscopic technology, will calculate your speed and distance covered. Then, by taking your weight into account, they will also give you an approximation of calories burnt. The figures for all of this will be displayed on the screen on your wrist and can be downloaded to your computer for analysis and archiving.

Rivals Nike have applied essentially the same technology in a hook up with Apple to allow the same information to be fed to you audibly through your iPod. In this case, you download and store the information from each run on your own page at **www.nikeplus.com**, where you plot your progress and chart your projections. Best of all, though, you can interact with other nikeplus community members in virtual race-type competitions as the info downloaded from your shoe sensors cannot lie.

Too much of a good thing

Although the advantages gained from making use of modern technology as you run are enormous, be careful not too get so caught up in it that you forget why you're there in the first place. It's easy to let splits timings, average speeds and target zones become a distraction and erode the simple pleasures to be gained from running pretty much for the sake of it. Also, if you let checking your phone or your wrist screen become too frequent during an event – and it's easily done – you can lose sight of the bigger picture and not end up running your best race. Every run is different and you will react differently to things that might appear to be the same; rather than attempt to regulate it with technology, it's usually more productive to simply go with that day's flow.

Before and after your run

Warming up and cooling down will be the most valuable 40 minutes of your running session

Don't be fooled into thinking that any time during your schedule not spent pounding the pavements is time wasted. No matter how keen you are to get running, don't neglect your warm up or cool down.

This section will show you exactly how much difference they can make to your performance and your enjoyment of running.

Warming up

Not warming up properly is probably the biggest single cause of athletic injuries. It's not rocket science – when cold, tight muscles are pitched into an intense workout, they cannot be expected to perform at a high level. Moreover, if they are pushed into it, something's going to give. In spite of such obvious logic, relatively few runners warm up diligently before every run.

Of course, with distance running, not warming up isn't going to be as potentially dangerous as it is for sprinting, as you can start off very slowly and work up your pace gradually. However, warming up isn't only about injury prevention. Warming up prepares you physically and mentally for the task ahead, thus a warmed-up runner will be able to give their best from the moment they hit the course. So, if you want to judge your performance accurately, a warm-up is very important, and it's absolutely crucial if you are about to start a race.

The purpose of a comprehensive warm-up is to bring your body and cardiovascular system up to the level they need to be at to perform most efficiently – known as race condition – but in a controlled and gradual way. A good warm-up should also incorporate some "dynamic" stretching to greatly reduce any chance of injury. This does not mean vigorously bouncing muscles – a sure-fire way of injuring yourself – but instead moving your joints in gentle movements to loosen the connective tissue (see p.82). Ideally, your warm-up should take 20–25 minutes, and involve five or ten minutes of pulse warmers, ten minutes of dynamic stretching and five minutes of run-outs.

- **Pulse warming** is the basis of any good warm-up, and consists of light jogging that slowly increases in speed, on-the-spot running or star jumps – anything to get the pulse rate up, hence the name. The idea is to slowly raise the body's internal temperature to a

> **❝** For me, warming up is essential. The secret of life is blood supply. Being deprived of it leads to gangrene. Warming up is intended to engage your blood supply and start to open up the tiny blood vessels – capillaries – that are the life force for every cell in your body. **❞**
>
> **Barrie Savory D.O.**

couple of degrees above normal. This will increase your heart rate, while your breathing will rise steadily to deliver more oxygen around your system. Blood flow will increase as the supply is diverted from internal organs to active tissue, where it will be carried by the expanded blood vessels in warmed muscles and tendons. This action in itself will raise your metabolic rate, causing your heart rate to rise further. Because warmed muscles are less dense than cold muscles, the contraction and expansion of tissue as you take your strides can take place at a greater speed.

- **Dynamic stretching** is a series of slow, deliberate movements designed to increase your mobility and loosen you up so that your muscles are ready when you start working hard. These exercises will reduce your "muscle stiffness", a term that refers to the ratio between the change in a muscle's length as it contracts and the degree of internal resistance to that contraction. The smaller the ratio, the smaller the likelihood of tearing, spraining or straining, which make up the vast majority of "didn't bother to warm up" injuries. There is more information on dynamic stretching on pp.82–89, including a range of dynamic stretching routines.

> It is vital you carry out pulse warmers before any dynamic stretching, as cold muscles are easily sprained or torn

Beat the oxygen gap

Warming up properly will counteract what is known as the "oxygen gap", the breathlessness experienced after your first burst of intense activity. It occurs because your bloodstream cannot deliver as much oxygen as the exerted muscles need, and you will gasp to take in extra air as a result – it's where the term "second wind" comes from. Correct warm-up procedures mean the flow of oxygen has been increased relative to muscle activity.

- **Stride outs** are the runner's version of the kind of skills rehearsal that sees cricketers whacking imaginary cover drives on the way to the crease or footballers taking air shots in the minutes before kick-off. They activate "muscle memory", which is a series of electrical impulses that have been almost engraved on the body's nerve paths as a frequently repeated physical action is recorded in the brain. This process ensures that movements are performed as instinctive reflexes rather than as a conscious process. To do stride outs, a distance runner would suddenly raise his speed from a gentle jog to race pace and hold that for 40–50 metres, then slow down for another 100 metres, and repeat the process about half a dozen times. For sprinters, stride outs will mean exploding into sprint speed for about a dozen paces, and practising sprint starts.

As important as the physical aspects of warming up are, you shouldn't neglect the psychological value either. Time spent warming up before a race or an intense training session should be time away from distractions, a period when you can put yourself in a running frame of mind and focus on what it is you want to achieve from that run. This concentration will also help your body's preparation as you will literally be psyching up your muscles for the effort that is to come.

Fact: Warming up and pre-race stretching will be much more important for a sprinter than for a distance runner – they have no time to ease into what they will be doing, as explosive, efficient muscle contractions will be required from the gun. It's a rule of thumb that the shorter your distance, the more attention you need to pay to preparation.

Cooling down

Also known as "warming down", this is probably the most neglected aspect of any sort of training routine, not least running. While failing to cool down properly after intense activity is unlikely to cause you permanent damage, it can cause considerable discomfort both straight away and in a few hours, and it can have an effect on your next run. Cooling down consists of getting your system back to normal in a gentle fashion, and doing some static stretching.

DOMS and the cool down

There's conflicting opinion in the running world as to whether cooling down reduces your chances of Delayed Onset Muscle Soreness (see p.179). Personally I don't believe it does, and recent research has shown DOMS to be the result of damaged muscles, not a standing excess of waste products. Also, DOMS occurs between 24 and 72 hours after intense exercise and those waste products would have dispersed within 12 hours by themselves.

Fact: Don't forget that the extra mile you cover as you cool down will count towards any distance you are entering in your training log.

Essentially, cooling down is warming up in reverse, and the main purpose is to reduce your heart rate and breathing after the intense levels they reached during exercise. The best way for a distance runner to do this is also the simplest – tail off and slow to a gentle jog for about three quarters of a mile (10 minutes) and then reduce that to a decreasingly brisk walk for another five minutes. A sprinter should continue jogging around the track until their heartbeat and breathing levels fall significantly.

As your cardiovascular system normalizes, you will stop producing large amounts of adrenaline, which will assist in lowering your heart rate. Slowing down your circulation will also keep blood moving through your veins and prevent it from collecting in the extremities, which can cause dizziness. Your breathing will slow as the need for extra oxygen in your bloodstream progressively drops.

This tapering off will also get rid of any unused lactate in the muscles in a very controlled fashion. If you just stop dead, any extra lactate produced in anticipation of great effort will stay in the muscles where it will become lactic acid and cause stiffness. Cooling down gradually reduces the amount of lactate produced, and at the same time ensures the pulse rate is sufficient to pump away any waste products that might have remained in the muscle tissue had you simply stopped short.

After you have wound down to a stop, spend 10 or 15 minutes performing static stretches (see pp.86–88 for a static stretching routine). While this stretching will assist with the removal of waste products from your muscles, the real advantage will be felt in the future, as static stretches elongate and loosen muscles and increase the range of motion permitted by the joints. Stretching in this way is cumulative, and it will permanently increase your muscles' flexibility (as long as you stay active and stretching). Relaxed muscles perform better and are far less prone to injury than taut muscles, so look on stretching after a run as early preparation for your next.

Static stretching can be done at any time – in fact you should have a good stretch once a day – but muscles warmed up by running will be far more receptive to stretching, and it will help them relax by reducing natural tightening after exercise. If you are going to stretch during the day, for example after a few hours sitting at your desk, be sure to perform five minutes or so of pulse warmers first so that you are not stretching cold muscles.

The cool-down period is also an important psychological full stop on your run. Before you get back into the mundaneness of real life, you can contemplate what you've just done or seen and either savour the good bits or figure out what you need to do about any bad bits. You can enjoy a bit of post-run banter with your running buddies, and, most importantly, look forward to your next run.

> **//** The first thing I'd do after I'd got injured was to get a massage, because even if the injury wasn't treatable by massage – and so many were – it would tell me a great deal about the nature of the injury and how to deal with it. **//**
> **Hugh Jones**

Massage

One of the greatest ways to round off a hard run or a tough training session – after you've cooled down and stretched – is with a deep tissue massage (sometimes called a sports massage). Quite apart from leaving you feeling so relaxed you might have to starch your trousers before you can stand up, a massage will knead away any lingering waste products in your muscles, speeding up the healing time of any muscular and soft tissue injuries you might have incurred during your run. Regular massage will also reduce tightness and improve flexibility and the joint's range of motion.

The massage loosens muscle fibres further. This continues to increase the blood flow within the tissue, which greatly speeds up the repair of any tiny internal tears that might have occurred while you were running. Deep tissue massage is particularly good for breaking up old scar tissue that has "stuck" to surrounding tissue. If too much scar tissue is allowed to build up across the fibres it will have the effect of permanently tightening the muscle as it will eventually restrict movement. Regular massage will also realign the microscopic elements of the fibres that have been pushed out of place by incorrect running action. If unattended these will then rub and cause muscle discomfort – the average runner's action goes unnoticeably but significantly out of whack as they get tired.

These massages are called deep tissue massages as the therapist will work on the underlying, difficult-to-get-to muscles, rather than just the surface layers. This involves more direct deep pressure or friction and different manipulation techniques, and will probably see the therapist using elbows, reinforced fingers and the heel of the

> **Fact:** During a deep tissue massage, the pressure will be stronger than for a regular massage but it shouldn't be agony – everybody will respond differently, so tell the therapist if you are experiencing any pain.

How often should you get a massage?

As often as you can! If you have a partner with a magic touch – and they know what they're doing – you are very lucky and ought to get one after every run. Otherwise it's definitely worth regular runners investing in one a week; it should cost you no more than £40 ($75). Although you can make a perfectly adequate recovery by cooling down and stretching, have a massage and you will notice a world of difference, both immediately and over the next couple of days.

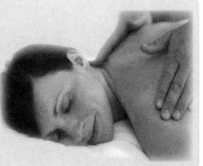

hand or foot rather than gentle soothing palm strokes. They will focus on specific joints, muscles or muscle groups, gradually easing in deeper to allow more movement. Very little oil will be used as the pressure doesn't travel much over the skin.

Stretching

Flexibility in both muscles and joints is important for any athlete, as it will enhance your performance and decrease the likelihood of

injury. For a distance runner, though, it is absolutely vital, as the nature of what we do shortens some of our muscles while we strengthen them, significantly increasing the risk of damage. Also, a runner can cope far better with the relentless impact from pounding the pavements if muscles and connective tissue are pliable, and a guaranteed way of improving your performance is to increase the mobility in your joints. The best way to achieve a

runner's necessary flexibility is with controlled stretching before and after your run.

The two main types of stretching you will need to concern yourself with: dynamic stretching and static stretching. A third method, ballistic stretching, is actually very popular – it was once the only type of stretching done in schools and gyms – but should be avoided at all costs as its potential for harm is enormous.

Dynamic stretching

This is mobility stretching and should be performed as the second stage of your warm-up routine. It involves moving your

Stretching dos and don'ts

✘ Never stretch a cold muscle – make sure you've performed a pulse-warming routine before you start

✔ Increase the mobility as you progress with the stretch

✘ Stretches shouldn't hurt. You should experience some mild discomfort as the muscle is pulled, but if that becomes painful, stop immediately as you are stretching too far

✘ Never bounce on a static stretch – ease gently into it

✔ Stay in control of the movement and your balance

✔ Make sure you are wearing clothes that will allow you to move and stretch freely

✘ Don't hold your breath while stretching – breathe slowly and evenly for maximum relaxation

✔ Create your own stretching routine as you decide what is best for you and the type of running you are doing

✔ Incorporate the time to stretch into your running schedule, so that it does not seem like an extra. This way it will stand less chance of being skimped on if you are short of time

✘ Don't stretch any muscle that has recently been strained or sprained, until you are 100 per cent sure it has recovered.

> There has been argument as to the true value of stretching, but I am a firm believer both as an ex-athlete and as an osteopath. It increases the range of joint motion, stimulates the muscle fibre contractile units, increases circulation, enhances the drainage mechanism and above all it simply feels good.
> **Barrie Savory D.O.**

joints in gently increasing movements to loosen connective tissue and wake the muscles up. Muscles and tendons are not pushed beyond a comfortable range with any great force; instead they are manoeuvred with gentle repetitive movement – for example a straightened leg will be swung backwards and forwards with the arc increasing slightly on each movement. A dynamically stretched runner will function much more efficiently at the start of their run than one who has skipped this process, as they will use less energy to produce the same movement.

Tip: The older you are, the more your muscles will lose natural elasticity, thus pre-run dynamic stretching becomes increasingly important.

A dynamic stretching routine

You should perform at least eight repetitions on each side, for each stretching exercise, but don't go mad as you won't get much extra benefit if you do more than twelve. Relax out of the stretch as soon as you feel resistance.

Body Part	Stretch no. 1	Stretch no. 2	Stretch no. 3
Neck	Standing straight, tuck your chin into your chest, then tip your head back as far as it will go.	Stand with head upright and lower your right ear to right shoulder. Bring it back to centre then lower your left ear to left shoulder.	Keeping your head upright, turn it to the left as far as you can. Turn back to face front, then turn as far as you can to the right.
Shoulders	Standing straight with arms loose at your sides, rotate your left shoulder, lifting it up to your ear at the top of the movement. After ten reps, repeat with right shoulder.	Stand straight with your arms loose at your sides, swing your right arm forwards to above your head while swinging your left arm back as far as it will go. Reverse the swings.	Standing straight with both arms outstretched to either side, swing your arms towards each other and across your chest. Swing out straight again.
Trunk	Stand with your feet apart and hands on hips. Raise your right arm over your head, bending sideways as far as possible to left. Return to upright, raise left arm, put right hand on hip and bend to right.	Stand with your feet apart and hands on hips. Rotate hips in a bump 'n' grind style clockwise ten times, then repeat ten times anti-clockwise.	

Hips	Stand with your left side next to some support, balance yourself with your left hand and stand on your right leg. Keeping left leg straight but not tense, swing it forwards and backwards as far as possible. After ten reps, turn and repeat with the right leg.	Stand facing a support, leaning forward slightly and balancing with both hands. Raise up on the ball of your left foot and swing your right leg across in front to your left, then back out to the right. Repeat ten times, changing legs.	
Knees	Stand with feet together, bend knees and place hands on them. Keeping head up and knees together, rotate knees ten times clockwise then ten times anti-clockwise.		
Ankles	Stand with feet shoulder width apart, supporting yourself on a wall (or tree) with both hands. Keeping legs straight, raise up at least three inches on the balls of your feet. Lower heels then repeat ten times.	By standing on one foot at a time, the ankles can be stretched individually, but make sure you still do ten reps for each.	

Tip: Many runners practise yoga or use power yoga movements as their static stretching, and maybe get even more benefit out of it.

Static stretching

Sometimes called passive stretching, as it does not involve repetitive movement, this is carried out after you run. You assume static positions then push gently to extend the muscle to its limit.

A static stretching routine

Breathing slowly and regularly, ease into each stretch there is increased resistance and some pulling sensation. Hold the stretch

for twenty seconds, relax and stretch once again on the same leg/side. The second stretch should feel more comfortable at the same distance, or you should stretch a little bit further. Exhale while you are stretching for the best results.

If you haven't got the time to perform all the stretches on every occasion, make sure your weekly programme incorporates them equally in rotation.

Fact: More than providing immediate benefits, over time static stretching will loosen your muscles to leave them much better equipped to handle the impact involved in road running.

Body part	Stretch
Feet and ankles	Sit on floor with legs out straight. Bring right foot back alongside left knee, resting on heel with toes pointing up.
	Keeping heel on floor, grab toes of left foot and ease back.
	Hold for twenty seconds.
	With heel remaining static, point same toes away from body.
	Hold for twenty seconds.
	Perform one more, repeat with other foot.

Achilles tendon	With feet shoulder width apart, step forward at least one metre with your left foot – your left thigh should be parallel to the ground, with shin at right angles.
	Keep your back leg straight with your back foot firmly on the ground and body upright.
	Resting hands lightly on your left thigh, move the knee forward until it is over your toes.
	Hold for twenty seconds.
	Relax by drawing the knee backwards.
	Perform one more, then repeat with other leg.
Calves	Stand with feet shoulder width apart.
	Keeping the heel on the floor, step your left foot straight back, lowering your hips to accommodate the longer stance and making sure your body remains upright.
	Stop when you feel the stretch in your calf, and hold for twenty seconds.
	Relax by returning the left foot back to centre.
	Perform one more, then repeat with other foot.
Quadriceps	Support yourself on something solid with your right hand.
	Standing with feet close together, raise your left heel backwards, keeping both knees parallel.
	Grab your left ankle with your left hand and gently pull the heel towards your buttock.
	Hold for twenty seconds.
	Loosen grip to relax.
	Perform one more, the repeat with the other foot.
Hamstrings	Sit with your legs out straight in front and feet together.
	Keeping your back straight, grab your ankles (or as far down your legs as you can reach).
	Pull your chest to your knees.
	Hold for twenty seconds.
	Loosen grip to relax and repeat.
	(Make sure to pull your chest, not the top of your head, to your knees as this will make sure your spine isn't curving and that the stretch pulls your hamstrings not your back.)

Fact: "No pain, no gain" is total nonsense. The whole reason we have pain is to tell us something isn't right; it is crucial to recognize this when doing any kind of stretching.

Groin	Sit on the floor with the soles of your feet together and heels pulled up towards your groin.
	With your knees pointing outwards, hold your ankles so that your forearms are along your calves and your elbows are resting on the inside of knees.
	Push down gently with elbows. Don't bounce.
	Hold for twenty seconds then repeat.
Iliotibial band (The thick strip of connective tissue running from knee to hip, on the outside of the thigh between the hamstrings and quads)	Sit on the ground with your left leg out straight in front and your right foot planted firmly on outside of the left knee.
	Twist your trunk to the right, placing your left elbow on the outside of your bent right knee.
	Using the elbow, gently push your right knee to the left – this will stretch the iliotibial band in the right leg.
	Hold for twenty seconds.
	Relax elbow pressure.
	Perform one more, then repeat with other leg.
Hips and glutes	Lie on your back with your legs out straight.
	Bend your right leg and raise until your right shin is parallel to the ground and at right angles with the raised thigh.
	Place your left hand on the outside of your right knee and, keeping as much of your back on the ground as possible, pull your right leg across your left leg until the inside of your right knee is on the ground.
	Hold for twenty seconds then return right leg to centre and relax.
	Perform one more, then repeat with other leg.
Lower back	Kneel on all fours, keeping your arms straight and below your shoulders, and your back parallel to ground.
	Tighten your abdominal muscles while angling your pelvis forward, causing your back to arch – if you are doing it correctly you will feel a stretch from the top of your glutes into the small of your back.
	Hold for twenty seconds.
	Relax your abs then repeat.

Ballistic stretching

Back when less was understood about how muscles worked, ballistic stretching was commonplace, and practised enthusiastically by the "no pain, no gain" brigade as the potential for participant agony was always considerable. Nowadays, we know enough to know it has no place in the sensible runner's routine.

Essentially, it is a combination of static and dynamic stretching in that it involves many of the former's poses, but moves like the latter as you are expected to jerk into a stretch, then elongate it by bouncing or pushing further into it a prescribed number of times. That is where all the problems will arise. If you throw your body weight into a stretch with no control, all the strain will be taken by the fibres of the muscle you are attempting to stretch, and all too often the muscle will tear.

Ballistic stretching will never be as effective as dynamic or static stretching, because this dangerous method can activate the muscle's internal defence system, the muscle spindles. Deep within the fibres, these spindles react to how far a muscle is being stretched and if it seems too far, they activate the myotatic or stretch reflex, which tenses the muscle to prevent further elongation. This will happen involuntarily, meaning that instead of loosening the muscle you will actually be making it tighter.

One foot in front of the other

Big steps forward

Running? Pah!
What's there to learn?
If you can walk, you can run.

That's perfectly true. But if you want to do it faster, for longer and without suffering too many injuries, there's quite a lot you ought to learn.

You now know what you need in order to run. This section looks at *how* to run. While it will get newbies started in the best way possible, it will also help experienced runners in that quest to achieve that little bit extra.

Action, man

Think of the running action as like hopping from foot to foot, and with each hop swinging the raised foot forward to land in front of the other foot. A hop with one leg and the corresponding movement of the other equals a running step; two steps – ie each leg has a hop – amounts to a stride. The sort of running we want to do is, of course, slightly more sophisticated than this, with the aim being to get through a stride as fluently as possible, delivering the maximum amount of forward momentum for the minimum of effort.

Firstly, it's important to note that there is no such thing as the perfect running technique, just like there is no "best" running shoe (see p.42). Because of the differences between runners in terms of size, weight, age, gender, muscle density, strength and so on, everybody's ideal stride will be unique to them. But there are theories and guidelines that can be universally applied, although they will probably need to be customized to fit your individual action.

The stride cycle

To analyse and improve your stride, you need to break it down into its component parts: the support phase, the drive phase and the recovery phase.

The support phase (aka the stance phase)

This is when your foot is actually in contact with the ground. In the best actions, initial contact is made by the middle of the foot, not the heel. The foot should start to strike slightly ahead of your centre of gravity so that when firm contact is made it will be directly underneath it. To cushion the impact of the landing, the knee joint should not straighten completely and the pelvis will dip slightly on the opposite side from that leg. As soon as the foot touches down,

Tip: Rather than stepping further forwards to gain momentum and stride length, concentrate on producing a firmer push back with the foot that is on the ground. That way, you will be much less likely to over-extend your stride.

contact is rolled forwards towards the toes. This action is supported by the iliotibial band in the leg that has landed and the core muscles, which provide some resistance to the body's cushioning of the strike and hold up your trunk as the centre of gravity shifts forward past the standing foot.

The drive phase

As the contact with the ground is rolled forward towards the toes the drive phase begins. The standing leg straightens, pushing backwards and downwards and extending the hamstrings and glutes. Then, as an additional lever, the foot is pushed off as the calf muscles straighten out the ankle. In an ideal stride this will provide force upwards along the straight leg towards the runner's centre of gravity in the hips. This should supply

As you learn how to run efficiently, the chances are you'll have to unlearn how you've been running since you were in nursery school.

enough vertical force to keep you upright when your centre of gravity is a long way in front of your foot or there is no contact with the ground, but it should take as little energy as possible away from the horizontal force which is what is driving you forwards. How much the ankle should flex as the foot leaves the ground depends on the style of running and how high the foot is going to be lifted: distance runners should stay close to the ground, meaning the ankle will stay almost rigid, while sprinters will virtually point their toes for much greater foot lifts of up to ninety degrees.

Type of running	Where foot should strike
Sprinting	Ball of foot/underside of toes
Short/middle distance	Forefoot/ball of foot
Long distance	Midfoot
Competition-pace long distance	Just in front of midfoot

Fact: Running differs from fast walking because, to walk, one foot must be on the ground before the other one is raised up from it. When running, both feet are off the ground during every stride.

Stride cycle 1-2-3

1. Support

Middle of sole of foot in contact with ground, knee and ankle flexed for shock absorption.

2. Drive

Rolling forward on the toes, pushing down and backward into ground to straighten the leg. Elastic recoil bends leg to move foot upwards and forwards.

3. Recovery

Heel moves towards the buttock, hips swing the leg forward and momentum starts to unfold the knee so the leg is almost straight when foot strikes and we're back at the support phase.

Tip: To practise rotating your hips, imagine them as a bucket full to the brim with water. As the angle of your torso changes, you have to keep from spilling the water, thus rotate your hips to make sure they stay level.

The recovery phase

As soon as the foot has left the ground, the leg begins the recovery, or swing, phase. As the foot lifts it will be behind the body, and the leg will raise, bend and kick forwards ready to come down and repeat the cycle. The most efficient runners will make this happen through a combination of muscle force, elastic recoil (see box opposite) and momentum left over from the drive phase. The hip flexors and hamstrings lift the leg, while the quads bend it so the heel heads towards the corresponding buttock, and the momentum carried over from the push from the ground swings the thigh forwards. As long as the quads are nice and loose, as the thigh slows down, the lower leg continues to move, pivoting at the knee joint to all but straighten the leg before the foot is put down.

Like riding a bike…

Good running begins in the trunk and in the hips, and is a smooth circular motion rather than a swinging pendulum – your feet ought to be moving as if you are riding a bicycle rather than taking a speedy stroll. All leg joints – hips, knees and ankles – need to be as loose and as flexible as possible to facilitate what should be that smooth circular motion.

The hinges around which the legs pivot are the hips, with the glutes, hamstrings and quadriceps controlling the action – this is why core strength is vital, because these huge muscles can only function properly if whatever is anchoring them isn't going to be pulled all over the place. After the foot strikes and pushes off, it will be drawn up and backward, to create the back edge of the circle. At first glance, this foot lift seems counter-productive and a waste of energy, but it isn't: by pulling the heel up towards the buttock, the arc that the foot has to travel is much smaller, therefore it can get round it quicker and with less energy expended. Getting it up there

Elastic recoil

Think of a rubber band being stretched to its limit and released. The energy created as it contracts is enough to launch a folded paper pellet all the way across the classroom. As you run, your legs work in exactly the same way, with the muscles within them functioning just like that makeshift catapult: they are stretched all the way then contract during the first phase of the recovery cycle, creating an explosion of energy. This is elastic recoil, and it amounts to free energy inasmuch as it requires no muscle exertion to create it.

To fully utilize this energy within your stride cycle it has to be released at the right time, the moment the sole of the foot lifts off from the ground. This means the leg has to remain almost straight while in contact with the ground; if the knee starts bending while the foot is still planted, the energy will be wasted, as elastic recoil will take place slowly and weakly. This timing is also important to create a forward rather than an upward momentum as the muscles contract to bend the knee, because the movement is carried through to form the top part of the foot's circular motion.

Muscle flexibility and joint suppleness aid elastic recoil enormously and, if fully exploited, can result in a faster turnover and considerable improvement in running economy (see p.112).

doesn't use much power either, as the hamstrings' natural reaction to being straightened during the drive phase is to contract, which bends the knee and pulls the foot up. The hip continues to rotate as the knee pushes forward and drops down to trace the front half of the stride's circle, and when the lower leg kicks out the hip joint on that side will be fully flexed.

Straighten up

The right posture is essential to successful running, helping you maintain energy efficiency and stay injury-free. Good posture will make sure everything is pointing in the right direction along all

Tip: If your chin is jutting forward, your head has gone past upright and is now too far back.

Fact: Good core strength will help you achieve and maintain an upright posture.

three axes so no effort is being wasted. It will also minimize joint and tendon impact and stress. Yet it is one of the most neglected areas of most new runners' training regimes.

A good posture begins with a straight back and an upright carriage, meaning that the spine should be vertical all the way into the neck and that your head should be held erect. This might feel slightly awkward, as if your head is tilting back slightly, but this is because most people's natural posture tilts their head forward. Try the eye line test: you should be focused on a point about 40 metres away, not on your feet or the ground directly in front of you. A straight back will keep you balanced, minimizing stress on your lower back and allowing your diaphragm room to operate, which means breathing will be much more relaxed.

However, an erect spine should not be achieved by tensing up your back and shoulders, and only a small proportion of runners will be able to keep ramrod-straight naturally. Rather than hold yourself

Run tall

When running with a straight back you should be as tall as possible to minimize pressure on your diaphragm. To achieve this position, take as deep a breath as possible, lifting your whole upper body, then hold that position after you exhale.

Body part	Ideal running posture
Head and neck	Erect, eye line focused about 40 metres in front, neck in line with spine.
Shoulders	Square to the front, level and loose; they should not move as you swing your arms.
Arms	Close into sides, elbows bent at approximately ninety degrees. Your arms should swing backwards and forwards, loosely from the shoulders in a natural arc – neither hand nor elbow should swing behind the line of the body.
Hands	Loosely rolled into fists, thumb resting on top of index finger, wrists straight and relaxed.
Trunk	Upright and facing forward, with chest out – if your head and upper back are positioned properly, your trunk will naturally fall into its correct place.
Hips	In line with shoulders; no lateral movement.
Legs	Working in a smooth circular action; knees shouldn't be lifted too high – sprinters will lift much higher than distance runners; no lateral movement.
Feet	Pointed straight out to the front so the energy of the push off is used as efficiently as possible. Avoid either slapping your feet down or landing heavily on your heels.

stiffly, lean forward very slightly so your upper body is relaxed, but make sure the angle is no more than a couple of degrees. If you are tense on top, you will not be able to let your arms swing almost by themselves, and you will have to put effort into any movement as you fight against tense shoulders.

Leaning too far forward is a common problem among new runners, simply because the upright position often feels unnatural. But putting your upper body out of kilter by angling it at the waist can cause a great deal of problems. It will throw you off balance,

Tip: Should you feel your shoulders either tightening or moving upwards, shake them out with your arms to loosen them and allow them to return to their ideal position.

meaning you will need to over-stride to stay on your feet, and that will put huge strain on your knees because your lower leg will be out of line as the striking foot lands. Leaning too far forward means unnecessary energy has to be used to pull you through your stride's support phase and greater effort will be required to support the upper body. It will also expose your lower back to added strain as each stride's impact will be felt more acutely.

Leaning back too far is much less common – it usually comes with fatigue – but is equally disadvantageous. Quite apart from the balance issues, it will put added strain on your stomach muscles by stretching them. It will also stress the base and top of your spine, curling them both over – the base because it has to accommodate the torso's angle, and the top from having to lower your head to see where you're going. It will constrict your diaphragm to a greater degree than leaning too far forward, meaning breathing will become difficult and tiredness will increase as the muscles' oxygen supply falls off. Also, leaning back plays havoc with your stride pattern, as you will have less control over where you put your feet down and your steps will become irregular.

Over-striding

After worn-out shoes and failure to warm up properly, over-striding is the biggest threat to running performance, a factor which increases considerably among novices. It's very tempting to stride out too far as a way of either conserving energy by decreasing turnover (see p.96) or increasing your speed by covering more ground, but in both cases over-striding will have the opposite effect.

If your foot lands too far in front of your hips (your body's centre of gravity), it will put unnecessary strain on your knees and hips, as the impact of landing will not be absorbed in a vertical line from

Four basic rules for running faster

1. Bend the knee on your swing phase; it will get to where it needs to be more quickly because your foot has to travel in a shorter arc.

2. Keep the muscles along the front of your leg loose (quads, hip flexors), so there is no resistance when you straighten your leg as you push off from the ground.

3. As you push off, consciously push backwards, getting the most out of your hamstrings and glutes. This will keep you moving forward rather than wasting energy going up and down.

4. Don't overbend the corresponding knee as each foot hits the ground. It will dissipate energy, dampen your elastic recoil and keep your foot in contact with the ground for too long.

Tip: To quicken your pace, speed up your turnover to increase your stride-per-minute rate to one hundred or more. Whatever you do, don't lengthen your stride.

the feet up through the ankles and knees to the hips. The knees will bear most of this unabsorbed shock as they are the pivotal point between the planted lower leg and the still-moving upper leg, but the iliotibial band will also suffer because the jolting involved will create all sorts of friction around your hips. Because over-striding pushes you to land on your heels, they will also take a bashing, as will your Achilles tendon.

Your performance will be affected in terms of both speed and endurance. Because of the jarring from landing on your heels, and your centre of gravity having to catch up with your lower leg, you are effectively putting the brakes on. The jolt stops your stride cycle being smooth enough to gain maximum momentum, and in the time it takes the foot to roll from heel to ball, the elastic recoil energy will be lost and you will be expending energy for a much greater proportion of each stride.

To avoid over-striding, practise your stride with gentle running and stride-outs, making sure to land on your midfoot, with a smooth forward momentum and very little jolting. Shorten your stride if you have to – the average runner should be taking between 85 and 95 strides a minute; much less than that suggests you are over-striding – then, if you want to cover more ground, increase your time in the air without overstretching your leading leg.

Up and down hills

Unless you plan to do all your running in Holland, sooner or later you're going to have to run up a hill and, very probably, down the other side. If technique is important on the flat, then it is vital on the inclines, and knowing how to run hills separates the good runners from the *very* good runners.

Correct technique on hills will gain you ground, conserve your energy and reduce the risk of injury. The only problem is that good hill running means employing techniques that will seem very different from the ones you've worked hard to master for running efficiently on the flat, and – in the case of running downhill – conquering one very natural fear.

Running uphill

The most important aspect of good uphill running technique is that it will conserve energy, which will pay back later in the run. Running uphill uses pretty much the same techniques and muscles as correct flat-surface running; the difference is the direction in which the effort is applied.

The most common mistake made by runners on an uphill surface is to stride out to maintain the same speed as on the flat by pushing harder against the ground. With this comes all the problems inherent with over-striding (see p.100), and the additional force being applied to the push will quickly drain you at a time when you need energy the most. Shorten your stride when running up hills, reducing your arm action correspondingly, and maintain the

Tip: As you go over the brow of a hill don't accelerate suddenly, but maintain total control over your running by easing into the faster pace and longer strides.

Tip: When running up a hill, just as your stride turnover should remain unaltered from running on the flat, so your breathing should stay the same. If it gets much heavier, then you are probably running too fast.

same stride per minute rate you would have on the flat. You should bounce up hills in short sharp steps, making sure you keep your elastic recoil at its most efficient.

I previously stressed the advantages of eliminating as much vertical body movement as possible from your stride, but when running uphill you need to gain height, thus some vertical movement is naturally required. The key is in an altered support phase (see p.94). Because of your shortened stride and the gradient of the slope, your foot will hit the ground sooner than on the flat and your knee will be slightly more bent, therefore your foot's movement should incorporate pushing down as well as pulling back. This will compensate for any decrease in elastic recoil that results from the reduced time and space available for the leg muscles to straighten pre-foot strike. It will also provide the momentum for the required vertical movement.

big steps forward

Sustained hill running is excellent for developing your quads, as the knees will need to be raised slightly higher to facilitate this kick down – how much higher depends on the gradient, and a rule of thumb is that as one foot strikes the ground the other leg should rise until the knee is pointing to the top of the hill. But don't kick your legs up like a showgirl – your feet should remain close to the surface as it rises in front of you.

The angle of your body to the ground should change for running uphill. You should remain straight, but be angled forward towards the crest of the hill – don't worry, you'll soon get over the feeling that you're falling on your face! This may mean that to maintain balance your foot strike will begin just in front of your hips, but make sure this doesn't lead to over-striding and never hit the ground in front of your head.

Running downhill

The key to efficient running down hills is to allow gravity to do most of the work for you, but to achieve that you'll have to overcome a natural fear of hurtling downhill out of control. It will be worth it, though, because with the correct technique you'll be able to have quite a rest as you cruise down hills of all gradients. As with running uphill, getting it right is more about energy conservation than gaining ground on the rest of the field.

Once again, the easiest mistake to make when running down hills is to increase your stride length. This will happen if you push off horizontally, which, in conjunction with the surface falling away, will mean you end up almost leaping along. Quite apart from this being grossly energy-inefficient as you are using a large amount of energy to push yourself forward, it will mean gravity is working against you. After the propulsive force pushing you forward has dissipated, you are allowing gravity to pull your striking foot down to the surface from a greater height than is recommended, thus

Fact: The vast majority of runners will put in special uphill training sessions as it involves obvious hard work, but they will neglect to work on downhill technique as it doesn't appear to have any fitness gains. Make sure you pay attention to both.

massively increasing landing impact. The stresses caused to your ankles, knees and hips will be felt later in a long run, and will have a cumulative effect on your body during your running life.

Ideally, you should be taking smaller steps to remain in control and, while keeping your body straight, angle yourself slightly forward to allow your momentum to carry you along. The angle of your lean should be relative to the gradient of the hill, as you need to strive to maintain the same right angle between self and surface as you would when running on the flat. Touch down with your striking foot as lightly as you can to minimize wasted energy, then keep your feet as low to the ground as possible to maximize your momentum's forward thrust. This way you will be expending minimum effort to maintain your forward movement, as the only energy used should be for keeping your arms and legs moving and staying on balance.

In this correct downhill running position, your feet will strike slightly behind your hips, which is a root cause of the fear of overbalancing. You just have to get used to it, and start by trying to adopt this technique on gentle slopes, before building up to the steeper ones. If you feel you are going too fast, shorten your steps to bring things under control – don't lengthen them as a way of catching yourself.

The engine room

Think of your body as a car – it's got the best wheels and the slickest suspension, but it'll be useless if the motor doesn't run properly.

This chapter deals with what actually keeps your arms and legs powering along the pavement – the heart, the lungs and the metabolizing of all those carbs. What goes on in your cardiovascular system can have a massive effect on your performances, in terms of both speed and endurance.

The heart of everything

Everybody knows that your beating heart is at the, ahem, heart of everything you do, but as a runner a big, strong, efficiently working heart will be vital to achieving your maximum potential.

As the diagram opposite shows, the heart is responsible for taking oxygen from the lungs and delivering it to the muscles via the blood passing through your body's arterial/capillary network. It delivers oxygen to every cell in the body, but it's the working muscles that make the highest demands, and the harder they are expected to perform, the more oxygen they need to receive. Also, your muscle-to-body-mass ratio will increase as your running progresses and this will further add to the amount of oxygen needed. For this reason, all athletes need a heart large enough to pump sufficient blood around the body without the pressure dropping or the heart having to beat at a dangerously high rate per minute.

A distance runner needs this oxygenated blood to be delivered at a constant pace over an extended period of time, without any undue strain. The efficiency with which your heart can do this is known as your cardiovascular fitness. Endurance training develops your heart in much the same way as your legs: the increase in the amount of work it is expected to do makes it grow bigger. After all, your heart is a muscle just like your hamstrings – it's just one you can't do without.

A big strong athlete's heart should not beat any more quickly than an untrained person's but it will move more blood because the stroke volume will be larger – this is the volume of oxygenated blood pumped through the heart's left ventricle every time it beats. There will be a difference of around 25 per cent between the stroke volume of an average person and that of an endurance athlete because of the latter's proportionately larger heart. This is why athletes have lower resting heart rates (see p.16) than normal people, because each single beat moves a greater amount of blood.

Fact: Although your resting heart rate will get lower as you become fitter, your maximal heart rate will not rise. It will, however, reach that maximal rate much more quickly and with much less internal strain.

7. Carbon dioxide is exhaled into the atmosphere

1. Oxygen is inhaled from the air

6. Carbon dioxide is delivered to the lungs

2. The lungs transfer oxygen to the blood

The runner's cardiovascular cycle

5. Carbon dioxide is discharged into the bloodstream

3. The heart pumps the oxygenated blood to the muscles and other organs

4. Working muscles use oxygen to burn glycogen, creating ATP (see p.110) to fuel movement

> **"** Running faster and further is all about training the relevant muscles to improve their function, and that improvement is largely due to increasing cardiovascular efficiency. Running up a flight of stairs will frequently result in that burning pain in the thighs that fatigues the muscles to a point of forced stop. This is the failure of the venous drainage system (the veins that flow away from the muscle) to clear the waste product of muscle energy consumption – lactic acid – from the stressed muscle fibres. Improvement in performance will arrive when the blood supply pump, the heart, can deliver more blood and the local blood vessels can more efficiently cope with clearing the lactic acid. **"**
> **Barrie Savory D.O.**

What's going on in your muscles

Your muscles' main source of fuel is glycogen or fat. In order for muscles to consume this fuel, oxygen has to be present to break it down and convert it into adenosine triphosphate (ATP), a chemical compound which is the form of energy that muscle cells need in order to work.

The production of ATP leaves by-products in the form of carbon dioxide (CO_2) and lactate. The carbon dioxide-laden blood is pumped back to the lungs, where the CO_2 is extracted and exhaled into the atmosphere. The lactate is also removed from the muscles by the venous blood flow and delivered to the liver where it is converted into glucose.

As the intensity of your running increases your muscles will be working harder and will need to metabolize glycogen or fat at a proportionally faster rate. Your system will have to increase the input of oxygen to achieve this. Hence the heavy breathing or gasping for air during and after hard workouts.

Your heart won't be cheatin'

When you are running, your heart should be beating at between sixty and eighty per cent of its maximal rate, fluctuating according to the intensity of your running. If you keep it beating at this level, you'll be pushing your heart hard enough to reap all the benefits of having a good workout but not so hard that you'll be putting it under stress.

Your heart rate is not necessarily related to what speed you are running at because your heart will be registering all sorts of extraneous factors – how stressful a day you've had, what the temperature is, how much coffee you've put away, if you're sickening for something – and will adjust itself accordingly.

Find your maximal heart rate

Your maximal heart rate (HR max) is the highest number of times your heart will beat per minute before it plateaus. Ideally, you should be running at between sixty and eighty per cent of it, so you will need to know how to work out what it is. Either use a heart-rate monitor or manually take your pulse at your wrist.

To find your maximal heart rate, simply run fast then check your beats per minute. Several times. Like this: warm up thoroughly, run easily for ten minutes then perform four twenty-second sprints with thirty seconds' recovery running in between. Run easy for thirty seconds then run at your top sustainable speed for two minutes. Take your pulse. Run easy for at least ten minutes then repeat the exercise twice, taking your pulse at the end of each session. The three figures should be within a couple of beats per minute of each other, and you can assume their average to be your maximal heart rate.

There are formulas for working your HR max – the most widely used is to subtract your age from 220 – but such set reckonings are no more reliable than the BMI index calculator (see p.17). In fact, relying on such formulas can be dangerous, as they assume that everybody of the same age will have the same HR max, whereas in reality they could vary by up to thirty beats per minute. So, even if the formula puts you in the middle of your age bracket, you could still be fifteen bpm or around eight per cent off what it actually is.

VO₂ to the max

The amount of oxygen you can consume while working out intensely is known as your aerobic capacity, or VO_2 max. This is a measurement of the maximum number of millilitres of oxygen, per kilogram of body weight, that you can use up in a minute – the

Tip: If you run with a heart-rate monitor, set it to beep at whatever you've calculated sixty and eighty per cent of your HR max to be. That way, if you stray outside it, it will let you know.

// When I'm running intervals with people and I want to get their VO_2 levels up I tell them "Run like somebody nicked your bag!" That usually gets them going. //
Efua Baker

Active recovery

This is pretty much what it says on the tin – recovering from a race with a short session of exercise at roughly thirty per cent of VO_2 max, instead of just stopping and lying down. It's really just another name for cooling down. Active recovery will speed the removal of excess lactate and actually facilitate faster muscle repair. It also provides a good psychological ending to the rigours of racing or training hard.

> *Concentrate on breathing out. Focus on timing your exhalation into the rhythm of your running so that you're breathing out every fourth step. Let the breathing in take care of itself – it always does! Then keep that breathing pattern whatever pace you're doing.*
>
> **Efua Baker**

higher the better. This is another indicator of how fit you are, and, just like your HR max, you can work to improve it.

A previously sedentary novice runner who has completed our first and second phase training schedules (see pp.18–20) should be doing at least 25 kilometres a week and, during those two months, their VO_2 max will have increased by twenty per cent. The next month, taking their distance up to maybe forty kilometres a week will see a further five per cent increase, and if you progress to eighty kilometres a week you can expect to add a further ten per cent. However, this will probably be close to your capacity as once you start increasing the distance beyond that, the improvement ratio drops dramatically and there will be very little to be gained. Research has shown that VO_2 max tends to peak at between eighty and one hundred kilometres a week.

For any programme of VO_2 improvement to be effective, though, your running intensity has to remain constant as your distances get longer. Optimum intensity for your training runs will be around seventy per cent of your maximal heart rate, with one twenty-minute stretch of 80 to 85 per cent per session.

Running economy

Your running economy is another important figure to understand. It is the percentage of your VO_2 max that you're using to achieve a particular speed – the smaller the figure, the lower your oxygen use and the greater your running economy. Good economy means you can then step up the pace or the distance and still remain well within your capabilities.

Your running economy will get better naturally as you train regularly and build up your strength. It can be worked on by improving your technique so as not to waste any energy in your stride, and by building up your strength – many distance runners do strength training simply to maintain a good level of running economy.

Carbs on call

Once you start running, all that carbohydrate you've been eating is broken down in your digestive system to extract glucose and glycogen. Glucose will supply immediate energy needs and will combine with oxygen to be burnt pretty much as soon as it arrives in your system. Glycogen, however, is stored in the muscles and in the liver to be converted into glucose and then ATP as required in the future. Around two-thirds of the body's glycogen reserves will be stored in the muscles and one-third in the liver.

Because glucose is vital for producing ATP, distance runners need to store as much glycogen as possible. Increasing your training runs will naturally increase your capacity, but 2,000 kcal will be about the most you can store – no matter how fit you are. The reason so

Calorific value

A calorie (cal) is a unit of measurement for the energy needed to raise the temperature of one gram of water by 1°C.

A kilo calorie (kcal or C) is equivalent to 1,000 calories. This is the measurement used on food packaging to denote the amount of energy that will be provided by a particular food.

many marathoners hit the wall at twenty miles is because energy consumption on a distance run will be around 100 kcal per mile.

Crossing the lactate threshold

The by-product of converting glucose into ATP is lactate, or lactic acid. For years this was believed to be the cause of post-run muscle soreness, but recent research has shown that lactate breaks down into mainly CO_2 and water, which is removed by the bloodstream, while the remaining 25 per cent of it gets synthesized into glycogen and glucose in the liver to be consumed as "free" energy. And after you stop running, it doesn't hang about in your system long enough to cause you any lingering discomfort. However, excess lactate sloshing about in your muscles during intense exercise causes a burning sensation within them and, as it cuts down on the amount of oxygen your blood can transport, brings on premature fatigue. This build-up of excess lactacte occurs because when so much energy is used in a relatively short space of time more lactate will be produced than can be pumped away. At this point you have crossed the lactate threshold (LT), and as it will be detrimental to your performance you need to make sure your threshold is as high as possible.

Raising your lactate threshold will allow you to run faster for longer, and is vital if you are going to race at distances of above fifteen kilometres. It's not too difficult either. The idea is to run lengthy intervals at just above your lactate threshold pace – five kilometres, then two kilometres at recovery pace and repeat. After several sessions within a month, doing this will noticeably raise your threshold. Your LT pace will be just below race pace, so to top it, you'll need to move at as fast a pace as you can sustain over the distance – it's important not to start out too fast and then slow after a couple of kilometres. After you've run an LT interval, you should feel like you haven't got a lot of running left in you for that day.

Putting in the miles

Training to increase your running capacity is hardly rocket science.

You go running more often, build up your distances/time spent, and thus improve your strength and stamina.

As a result you'll be able to complete longer races, and finish shorter ones more quickly.

And there's nothing at all wrong with such methods – indeed, they work for the huge majority of runners. However, it doesn't need much more effort to take a slightly more scientific approach, one that will put you in far greater control of your progress.

Tip: Increase your speed on the short runs, but stay at your usual pace on the long runs, concentrating on maintaining that speed for the entire extended distance.

Fact: Long runs increase your aerobic abilities, and thus your VO$_2$ max, as any regular extended workout will multiply the number of oxygen-bearing capillaries in the muscles concerned.

Fact: Speed drills should only be undertaken by runners at a reasonable level of fitness, not complete beginners, as they can put intense strain on an out-of-condition body. For this reason, warming up is absolutely vital.

Tip: An ideal long and short scenario is to do two short runs during the week, either in the evening or early morning, and one long run at the weekend.

The long and short of it

Once you have decided to formalize your running, inasmuch as you want to achieve certain levels of ability or fitness or weight loss, the most immediately useful step you can take is to divide your runs up into "long" and "short". The latter will be your usual run, the former will be at least half as long again – two-thirds is the ideal addition, which can be in terms of time or distance covered. This formula should be applied to whatever the length of usual run, as it is about a relative rather than a linear increase in effort.

Create a schedule that means, at the very least, that one in five of your runs will be long, but the highest frequency should be one in three. This is because you will be pushing yourself, and will therefore need at least a week to recover between long runs – as a comparative exercise your regular runs will start to be viewed as rest periods! However, if you are doing any less than one long run every two weeks, progression will be lost and it'll be as if you are starting your plan from scratch each time.

The idea is that as the long runs become easier the short runs begin to seem almost negligible, so both can be extended, keeping the same proportions and frequency. This will increase your strength and endurance, as the tougher workouts build up muscles while your body will naturally start to increase its glycogen storage levels to cope with the additional demand. The longer runs can have quite dramatic effects on your weight, too. For example, a single one-hour run will burn more calories than two half-hour runs because you spend the same amount of time getting to the point at which you start burning calories (approximately fifteen minutes), thus you burn proportionately more on the hour-long run.

Mentally, long and short running is enormously helpful. If your short run is your regular racing distance, once you are used to the long run you will feel like you are handling races with ease, eliminating so many pre-race jitters and giving you the option to go a bit faster. Then the long runs can psychologically prepare you for longer races without the pressure of actually being in a race, while a controlled build-up to greater distances makes them a far less daunting prospect.

Speed training

Most distance runners focus on strength and endurance as being the keys to improvement, but this will often be at the expense of speed work. Running fast isn't only for sprinters, and the improvements it can bring to your performance will be absolutely vital if you are preparing for a race and have loftier ambitions than merely finishing the course. And, just as importantly, bombing along as fast as you can after months of slow, steady distance running is a great deal of fun and will bring an enjoyable change of routine to your training sessions.

Speed work is running at a pace of more or less twice your usual speed for a set time or distance, and it will prepare you for the higher levels you may need to rise to in competition, in a way that is far more effective than regular-pace running. It has important psychological considerations too, as it is easy for distance runners to slip into a running comfort zone which speed work jolts them out of. It makes them push on at a higher clip than they might be used to – race pace – and teaches them to maintain it while coping with whatever initial discomfort it might bring.

On the physical side, speed work prepares your system for an intensity of working that might not have occurred in your regular training runs. Because your turnover will be quicker, your legs receive a workout that should activate your fast twitch muscles, and the mechanics of your stride will sharpen up. Your cardiovascular

Tip: Once you are well into a long and short schedule, don't get worried about missing the occasional long run. If you feel you need the rest, it will do you more good than over-exerting yourself.

Don't look at the horizon – it can be demoralizing for a new runner because it constantly reminds them of how far they have still got to run. Focus on a spot several metres in front of you and imagine the road is a treadmill coming towards you.
Efua Baker

Fact: Sprinters work to increase their speed by performing short training runs – 50 metres or so – down hills. Using gravity as they run downhill is the only way they can get their limbs to move quicker than they would on the flat and so manage to train at faster than race pace, like a distance runner does with speed sessions.

> I always found interval training to be the most effective – that is, bursts of fast running to go into oxygen debt then slowing for recovery and repeating. The aim is to run faster, shorten the recovery time and then you are there. It is competing against your body and improving its efficiency.
> **Barrie Savory D.O.**

Tip: If you are running with a friend, the best way to incorporate speed routines as you go round your route is for one of you to turn around and run 30 paces back along the route while the other continues as normal. At 30 paces the first runner turns again and has to sprint at least 50 metres to catch the other up.

Tip: Always plan an interval session before you set out, then stick to it. That way you will get much more out of it and will have far greater awareness of your progress than if you attempt to make it up on the hoof.

fitness will improve rapidly, as you will have to take on board much greater quantities of oxygen and your heart will need to beat faster to deliver it. When you begin speed sessions, you will be panting and your pulse racing but, as you get into them, you soon notice this is no longer the case as your aerobic capacity increases to deal with these challenges. This is vital for 5k and 10k runners.

Most importantly, as your speed work takes effect, not only will your regular pace increase, but it will seem like a gentle jog in comparison with the sprints. While this does wonders for your starting line confidence, it also leaves you secure in the knowledge that you have speed in reserve as your secret weapon. Because your body is totally aware of how to run fast, at any point during the race you will be able to shift gears smoothly and accelerate. Or, when approaching the finish, you'll still have the energy and the mindset to be able call on that little bit extra.

However, you shouldn't speed train all year round as it will have a detrimental effect on your endurance and, as regards you getting faster, it will be subject to a law of diminishing returns. A distance runner should do no more than one speed session a week, raising that to two in the build-up to an event, and even then the fast bits should make up no more than five per cent of your total mileage.

Interval training

Interval training involves structured speed sessions and has been the basis of athletic and sports training for ages, with the same principles being applied to cycling, swimming, rowing and so on. For runners,

Speedy technique

The best way to run faster is to practise running more quickly than you'll need to. It's why sprinters practise explosive 20 or 30 metre dashes and marathon runners will train at 5k speed, but each will make sure they have perfect technique. If you can perform your stride's actions correctly at a higher pace, you will be able to do so much more efficiently at a lower speed. This conserves energy for long runs and the smoother movement allows a faster action, when needed, with far less effort. Running faster stimulates the motor neuron pathways so that muscle memory functions more efficiently at lower speeds, and keeps the joints and tissues loose and pliable.

When training at a higher speed it is crucial that you rigidly adhere to your regular style and *only run as fast as you can like that*. Altering your action to try to gain a bit of extra pace could be disastrous, because your brain will have two styles to sort out and it will apply whichever motor neuron pathway is carved the deepest – regardless of what type of run you are on.

Fact: Interval training is also acknowledged as a much better way to lose weight than slower, longer distances, as the intense running burns fat far more effectively.

Tip: It's best to do your interval sessions on a track, where you can accurately judge the distances you are covering, and so time yourself more precisely.

Tip: A heart-rate monitor is particularly useful for interval training to monitor recovery periods and assess the varying aerobic effect your training session is having on you.

Tip: If you can, perform stride-outs with a friend so you can observe and comment on each other's running technique.

the intervals concerned are alternate stretches of intense, faster-than-usual running and "recovery" periods during which you run at your normal pace or simply jog. Intervals are being increasingly utilized by sprinters, but have long been the mainstay of distance racers' schedules as they are sufficiently disciplined and formalized to allow them to plot improvement and set clear targets.

As well as working the aerobic system, interval training's high intensity stretches will push the anaerobic side of things, which is normally the preserve of sub-5k runners. During the fast phases your muscles' oxygen needs will be such that your cardiovascular rate will increase and you will start to tip over your lactate threshold, meaning you will be producing more lactic acid than can be moved away. This will raise your lactate threshold and increase your muscles' internal efficiency; it seldom occurs during long steady runs, and has to be achieved in regular short bursts.

Laddering

An interesting way to increase your intensity without doing yourself damage is to "ladder" your intervals. As the name suggests, this involves climbing up the levels of intensity by lengthening the fast stretches of your session, then climbing down again by decreasing them. A 10k runner might do two 200m fast runs, followed by two 500m, one 1k and finally a 1.5k; they would then come down with another 1k, two 500m and finally two more at 200m.

Fact: On strict interval sessions, recovery stretches between sprints should be kept to a minimum, as letting your heartbeat fall too far back towards normal will bring down average levels of oxygen consumption and lactate production, which will reduce your VO_2 max and lactate threshold.

Something for everybody

The beauty of interval training is that it is entirely flexible and you set the intervals yourself for whatever you want to achieve. Or even how you are feeling that day. When planning your programme, don't forget that speed is relative: what a 10k runner might term "fast" would be a snail's pace to a sprinter, while that same sprinter's speed training bursts could cause serious injury to the 10k runner and offer no improvement whatsoever to his performance. So plot your interval in relation to your race pace, or projected race pace, not strict timings.

Distance	Goal	Intense running	Recovery period
Sprinters (100m–800m)	Explosive acceleration, strength, highly active fast twitch muscles.	10 x 30m, flat out from start; 10 x 10–12 seconds, flat out from start.	One minute between each for complete recovery.
Middle distance (800m–3000m)	Anaerobic speed training to improve glycogen delivery and increase lactate threshold.	Between six and ten intervals of one third of race distance; at twice regular race pace.	Recovery stretches should be the same length of time (not distance!) as the fast bits.
Long distance (5k and upwards)	Aerobic improvement of VO_2 max; increase oxygen delivery to muscles over an extended period.	Sustained periods faster than race pace; 5 x 500m at twice race pace; 3 x 1 or 2k at 1 min/k faster than race pace.	Recovery stretches should be half as long as the speed interval.
Marathons	Improving stamina and VO_2 max.	5 x 1K at 5K race pace/3 x 3K at 10K race pace.	One minute/five minutes recovery running.

Fartlek

Invented in Sweden, this is an unstructured version of interval training – the name translates as "speed play" – and it can be great fun when out running by yourself. The concept is the same as the above – to alternate stretches of intense running with recovery stretches, but it's done on an ad hoc basis: sprint to that bench, then jog up the rest of the hill; sprint from one corner to the next, jog a block then sprint the next; try to get to the end of the road before that bus does… It can supply all the advantages of interval training, but doesn't need a track or a stopwatch and is so infinitely variable that it can make your regular route seem different every time. It is ideal for beginners who may not be ready for structured intervals, as they will get as intense a workout as they can cope with on the day.

Stride-outs

Stride-outs involve running between twenty and one hunndred metres at about 85 to 90 per cent of your top speed, relaxed and in perfect style. They can be interspersed in your run or done at the beginning or end and are skills-honing sessions to perfect your technique and impress the notion of running fast on your memory. This is vital because although movement will be committed to the body's motor neuron pathways, speed will not and if not practised frequently it will need to be re-remembered each time – watch sprinters training; they are almost constantly doing stride-outs.

As you perform your stride-outs, you should go through the complete range of motion on each step. This may appear exaggerated, but this is because on regular runs you have probably developed technique short cuts. Such an increased range of movement will give you greater functional flexibility in your muscles and show up flaws in your style far more vividly.

Seven speedy steps

1. Set an ambitious but not unrealistic goal – ten per cent improvement in the next three months.

2. Split your distance into shorter stretches and run them faster than your target time. If you aim to do 10k in 45 minutes, run single kilometres in under four.

3. As you progress, cut down the recovery periods but keep the intense speeds to what they were.

4. Speed work should only be part of a session, and the intense running should not take up more than a third of the total time.

5. Start off with no more than one speed session every three runs; maybe up it to two out of three when you are preparing for a race.

6. Stay stretched. When pushing your body under these conditions, stretching before and afterwards is vital, as is warming up.

7. Work on your overall fitness as you will need to achieve VO_2 max.

It's supposed to be fun!

Don't do all your running as intervals or speed sessions. About one in three sessions should be a regular longer-distance, lower-intensity affair, as this will allow recovery both physically and mentally, and will return you to running as relaxation.

// Once you get into a regular training schedule – such as if you're getting ready for a race – you'll find the routine of it develops its own momentum and that becomes enough motivation in itself. **//**
Hugh Jones

You can keep your training log and journal online. The following sites provide a free service.

www.coolrunning.com/log
www.nikerunning.com

The runner's training log

Training logs are the most multi-functional piece of kit any runner can own, as there is far more to them than simply using the successes of previous runs to motivate yourself for the next.

If you are starting out as a runner, filling in a log after every run will tangibly track your improvement and help you judge what you ought to be aiming for. Plus, it will allow you to look back and, from the notes you have written after each run, work out if you are over- or under-training. For the seasoned runner, training logs allow you to detect patterns in how you run at different times of the day, in different conditions and on different days. This allows you to work out how to get the most from your time spent running. If you are preparing for a race, the log can be completed in advance to create a mapped-out training schedule that can then be ticked off and commented on as it progresses.

It is very important to make the effort to fill your log in as soon as you get back from each run. It's very easy to forget details, and if you don't manage to fill it in a couple of times, you'll break the spell and stop using it.

All training logs are personal, and it will probably be best for you to construct your own, as only you will be able to decide what information is truly relevant. Use the example shown opposite as a guideline. A general rule is to chart as much information as possible, as factors such as weather conditions, time of day and pulse rate before and after the run will all contribute to the picture you want to build up about your running. But mostly logs are vital as something to look back on after you think you've done a particularly slow time on your regular circuit, to remind you just how fast it was compared to six months ago!

Week no.					Date
Day	Time	Distance	Timing	Pulse	Comments/observations
M					
T					
W					
T					
F					
S					
S					

Totals	WEEK	SCHEDULE	Overall comments
Distance			
Time			

❝ Strength training is often neglected by runners but it's absolutely vital in helping to improve your running and reduce injury risk. Core stability is also important to being able to run efficiently and to reducing injury risk. It's usually worth getting one-to-one instruction in both core and strength training as correct technique is vital. ❞

Karen Hancock

Strength training

Many distance runners are frightened of strength training, because they don't want to be saddled with carrying the extra weight that added muscle brings – muscle weighs more than fat. However, there's a huge difference between turning yourself into the Incredible Hulk and putting on the few kilos of lean muscle which will definitely help you as a runner.

Functional training – merely running to improve your running – is fine, but to get the best from your running you should train the body as a whole. This is because it works as a whole and even the muscles not directly applied to turning your stride over need to be strong to function in conjunction with the others. When correctly applied to running, strength training can vastly improve how your muscles work in concert – running is a series of concerted muscular exertions revolving around the body's core, meaning all-round strength permits greater running economy. Thus any increase in bulk will be minimal as you simply won't need it.

The key to efficient strength training is increasing core strength through developing the abdominal muscles and concentrating on the deep abs or transversus abdominis. These are the muscles behind the six pack that support the lower back, provide stability for the pelvis and connect to the diaphragm – the muscles that contract when you cough – and you should focus on them, to develop abdominal strength from the inside out. Well-developed deep abs will form a solid fulcrum for the legs to pivot from, meaning more control in your movement and less wasted energy on the push against the ground. A strong core will also keep your body aligned, meaning that you can maintain better posture for longer, stopping the base of the spine from slipping or moving and so preventing the lower back pain that plagues so many runners (see p.176).

Strength training will also improve your running efficiency by working your shoulders, upper arms and chest, which are muscles that can hugely help your technique if they are strong enough. It can also provide the muscle balance needed to counteract the developing of such "running muscles" as the hamstrings or the calves, by strengthening the muscles they work against in your running stride.

Before attempting the overall strength training programme below, read the guidelines on the right.

Exercise	Area worked	Movement	Amount	Progression
Crunch	Deep abdominals	Lie on back, arms across chest, knees drawn up. Lift shoulders by crunching abs towards pelvis.	Three sets of eight.	Increase number of reps, but stick to three sets.
Bridge	Lower back and glutes	Lie on back with knees drawn up, feet on floor, palms behind head on floor. Push down with hands and feet, raise pelvis and buttocks until back is straight. Hold for 30 seconds, relax and repeat.	One set of eight.	Increase the reps; lift alternate feet and straighten that leg while holding the bridge.
Plank	Core strength	Lie face down, support weight on forearms and toes, keep body straight and rigid. Hold for five seconds, relax on to knees.	Three sets of six; holding for five seconds.	Increase the length of the hold.

Strength rules

Warm up thoroughly beforehand.

Take a few minutes' rest between each set.

Drink water in between exercises – strength workouts can be surprisingly dehydrating.

Stretch after a strength workout.

Don't do a strength session on the same day as you run.

Don't do more than two strength sessions a week and never on consecutive days.

Exercise	Area worked	Movement	Amount	Progression
Superman	Back	Lie face down, legs and arms out straight. Raise shoulders, draw up one arm with elbow upwards. Raise outstretched arm and opposite leg 30cm – like Superman flying – hold for five seconds, repeat with other side.	Two sets of eight on each side.	Increase the time for which the pose is held.
Walking press-up	Shoulder strength; core stability	Assume top press-up position, with piece of card under toes so they slide. Keep back straight, walk across room with hands, then walk backwards to start position.	Cross room twice, with a minute's rest in between.	Walk for longer stretches; keep alternate feet raised.
Leg lift	Quadriceps	Sit on a chair with back straight and thighs parallel with floor. Raise one leg until straight; hold for five seconds. Relax and repeat with other leg.	Three sets of six.	Increase length of hold; do it with heavy shoes on.

Wide press-up	Shoulders, triceps, chest	Assume regular press-up position but with hands 30cm farther apart. Push up to arms' limit, then lower yourself until nose only touches floor and push up again.	Three sets of at least eight.	Place one foot on top of the other, or raise feet above head by resting on a chair or bench.
Dirty dog	Outer hip muscles	On hands and knees, with thighs and shins at right angles, lift one leg out to the side – think dog and lamp post! Hold five seconds, relax and repeat with other leg.	Three sets of eight.	Increase the reps; do it with heavy shoes on.

Tip: When selecting weight for an exercise, if you can't do more than ten repetitions straight off, it is too heavy.

Weighty matters

The strength training exercises above were selected because they can be done by anybody, anywhere, at any time (within reason), as the only equipment you need is a chair and a piece of cardboard. However, here's how to get the most out of training with weights:

1. Do as much as possible standing up, for balance and stability.

2. Train legs individually as much as possible, so your weak leg can't hide behind the strong one – and everybody will have a strong leg.

3. Concentrate on exercises that seem relevant to running movements – step-ups, lunges, single-arm rowing and so on.

4. Establish diagonal patterns as much as possible – ie opposite leg and arm – which imitate the natural running balance.

5. Opt for lighter weights and more, faster reps to avoid bulking up.

Weighted training

The other way weights can be used is to run wearing them. Literally. There's a range of weighted vests and wrist and ankle weights on the market for strength and endurance training in a number of sports, with the idea being that as you perform your discipline the extra weight strengthens exactly the muscles and tendons you will need. Also, there is the runners' method of leading up to a race doing training runs of the same distance wearing weights, then racing without them. Your body will have become accustomed to the extra weight and conditioned itself to perform carrying it, so on race day you will react as if that poundage is still there and, because it isn't, your performance and endurance will be considerably improved.

Weighted vests

These are not unlike Roman gladiator breastplates or police body armour, as they have to have a degree of rigidity to hold stable while you are running. Look for models that have been orthopaedically designed, as they will have an intrinsic back support to reduce the stress of carrying weights like this. A good vest should have many different pockets, to stop the load moving while running, to allow it to be distributed evenly and to be adjusted across a wide range – look for a vest with weights divided into 500g units.

For a snug-as-possible fit, the vest should be of "clamshell" design, hinging at the shoulders, and finely adjustable with vertical and lateral straps. It should have a moisture wicking lining, be breathable and have sufficient cushioning at all points of contact.

When starting to train with a weighted vest, you should not load it to a total weight of more than ten per cent of your body weight – not forgetting to include the weight of the vest. After half a dozen or so sessions, increase the load gradually – by a kilogram or so every couple of weeks – until you reach that advised maximum of ten per cent of your body weight.

Ankle and wrist weights

Ankle/wrist weights (the same can be worn on either) are padded straps with Velcro fastening, shaped to fit snugly and either filled with sand or shot of a fixed weight, or with sealable pouches to hold varying amounts of separate weights.

The theory used to be that they increased the likelihood of stress injuries to the knees or ankles, but this has been disproved recently and provided you build up gradually, ankle weights have been shown to improve leg strength and muscular power, while greatly increasing your calorific burn. For distance running, you should start with a pair of 500g weights and build up, in increments of 500g per ankle, to no more than 2.5kg on each leg. A heavier load can be applied if you are merely exercising – leg raises or slow stair steps for instance. As regards wearing them on your wrists while running, which will improve your overall aerobic conditioning, you could go up to five kilograms, but you will need to be very careful not to swing your arms too much as you could damage your shoulder or elbow joints.

Crosstraining

Supplementing your running programme with another activity is known as crosstraining, and it can benefit runners at every level. If you choose the right activity, crosstraining can boost your cardiovascular levels by providing a more intense workout than you might get from a run. Or, if you opt for an arm-centred sport like rowing or kayaking, you can enjoy upper-body strengthening

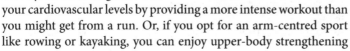

> Crosstraining is very important. Too often runners don't want to do anything that isn't actually running, but covering long distances each week can be very stressful, so to reduce the risk of injury you need to look for something that will maintain your fitness levels but will take you away from those stresses. Having another form of exercise will stop you going crazy too, especially if you're recovering from injury and can't run.
> **Karen Hancock**

Tip: On your weekly schedule, substitute one of your short runs for a 40-minute crosstraining session, building up the time spent as you progress at your new activity, then maybe add another session per week. But this shouldn't be at the expense of any more running.

Fact: Cross-country runners can benefit particularly from a crosstraining activity that involves some sort of lateral movement to build up the muscles that govern sideways stepping – like skating. Regular running doesn't work these muscles, but the uneven surfaces and jumping involved in cross-country will call on them frequently and unexpectedly.

you won't get from running. Marathon and other very long distance runners gain greatly from crosstraining as it can be used to redress the muscle imbalance that naturally occurs as a result of their schedules. And, importantly, taking on another activity is probably the best remedy there is for the boredom that can set in from running the same few routes time and time again.

If you are dealing with a running-related injury, a non-impact activity will allow you to maintain high levels of fitness while you recover. Being fit when you return to running reduces the chance of the injury recurring as you build up your distances.

Cycling
Although this gives you a leg workout, it primarily uses the front muscles – the quads and the shins – which running doesn't strengthen.

Cycling has great cardiovascular potential, and you have the boredom-busting choice of road or mountain biking.

Rowing and canoeing
Although this is good for developing the chest and shoulders, rowing (and canoeing and kayaking) is also very good for core strength as it works the abs, deep abs and back.

Swimming
Swimming is great for staying loose and for all-round conditioning, but has most effect on the upper body. Because it is non-impact and non-weight-bearing, it is ideal for runners recovering from an injury or not wanting to take risks before a race.

Skiing
Probably the riskiest crosstraining exercise you should be

Tip: If you're going to take up swimming and cycling as your crosstraining options, why not take them seriously and consider the triathlon?

considering, but highly worthwhile as it provides a whole-body workout and has huge aerobic potential.

Skating

This works much the same muscles as running, so if you have a muscular injury you won't be able to do this either. Its big advantage over running is its lateral movement that can strengthen the lateral rotator group of muscles and keep the iliotibial band flexible.

Yoga

The stretching and spine and hip lengthening in yoga is excellent for soft tissue flexibility and joint mobility. At the same time, it can provide a good source of strength training, as so many of the poses involve supporting or pushing against your own body weight.

10 tips for finding another sport

1. Start slowly – don't assume you'll be good at it just because you're a good runner.

2. Don't go for something that requires loads of expensive kit, just in case you don't get on with it.

3. Join a club or a class.

4. Pick something that will work muscles other than your running muscles.

5. Make sure it will actually give you the workout you require, otherwise you might as well be sitting at home. Or out running.

6. Try not to choose a contact sport (including football), as you will inevitably pick up knocks and this will interfere with your running.

7. Find out what the likelihood of injury is before you get into it.

8. Go for something non-impact – cycling or swimming or rowing – to give your joints a rest.

9. Do it with a friend.

10. Make sure it's something that's going to be fun.

Run safe

Personal safety when out running isn't very different to when you're out shopping.

There are lots of similarities, in fact. When read through as a list of dos and don'ts, runners' safety advice seems little more than an exercise in basic common sense. Yet you'd be surprised at how many apparently common-sense tips people just ignore.

What follows is mostly a reminder of things you are probably already aware of, plus a few runner-specific hazards that might not be so obvious.

General considerations

The golden rule is safety in numbers. Quite apart from the previously discussed benefits of a running buddy or two, if you are out running with other people, you are far less likely to get into any trouble. The most safety-conscious of the group will keep everybody else alert, and even if something does befall somebody, there will be other people who know them on hand to help or go and get assistance.

However, a recent survey in *Runner's World* magazine found that more than ninety per cent of the UK's runners run by themselves. The most important thing for those going solo is communication with the outside world. Tell somebody where and when you are going and roughly how long you expect to be – even if you deviate or opt for a longer run it will give people somewhere to start if you haven't come back after several hours. In addition, carry a mobile phone with you. Although many runners run to experience a couple of hours' freedom from their ring tones, this doesn't mean leaving your phone behind as, in extreme circumstances, it could save your life. The thing to do is keep it switched off unless you need it. Make sure you have the details that might be needed in an emergency on your person, in case you need help and are unable to give this information: name, contact number, blood group, medical specifications – see box below.

Tip: If you can't swim, it's never too clever to go running near water – canal tow paths, lakesides, river banks. You'd be amazed at how many runners find this out the hard way.

Tip: Always expect the unexpected, and be aware of the worst that could happen. Just because you feel safe doesn't mean you are safe.

Fact: The safest time to go out running is first thing in the morning, just after it has got light. There will be fewer cars or people about, in cities the pollution levels will be at their lowest, while in the country or on the beach the risk of thunderstorms will be smallest.

Make yourself a medical card

If you're going to run by yourself, print your name, your blood type, any relevant medical details and an emergency contact name and number on a piece of card and carry it with you each time you go out. If possible, take it to your local print shop to get it laminated and punched so that it won't get damaged while you run and you can wear it around your neck or wrist.

Vary the route of your run and the time at which you do it. Travelling the same route at the same time, day in, day out, can alert nefarious types to three things: you will always be in a certain place at a certain time with very few clothes on, and your house will be unattended for a specific amount of time, as will your car if you have driven to your run. Research shows that the vast majority of runners only ever run two or three routes, so mix them up as much as you can. If you are thinking of doing a new route, plan it properly beforehand to make sure there's no potential danger spots. If there are, at least you will be prepared for them. If you can, drive it or walk it first just to be sure, maybe with somebody else so you are less vulnerable. If, like many runners, you actually enjoy exploring on the hoof, try not to get hopelessly lost – check out the area on a map first to learn a few landmarks so you can give yourself at least some idea of where you might end up. You don't want to have to walk because you've no idea where you are, or stop a stranger to ask for directions.

Don't plan new runs through "dodgy" areas or shopping precincts after hours and, in spite of the potential embarrassment factor, stick to well-lit routes with an obvious pedestrian population and businesses that are open. Never set off for a cross-country run at dusk, away from street lamps – it can get dark scarily quickly.

Personal security

If you are verbally abused, derided or threatened while running, ignore it. This sort of loutish, casual intimidation is thoroughly unpleasant and all too common, but unlikely to escalate into anything more serious. Don't shy away from eye contact, as this will put you in victim mode, but don't return a look that is aggressive or provocative, and carry on running with the same pace and posture. Cross the road if it makes you feel safer when approaching what might be trouble and be prepared – without showing it – to sprint to get away.

> **Tip:** Be extra careful if you have to take a pit stop as you'll be at your most vulnerable. Don't use the same place on your run every time.

> **Tip:** Websites such as **www.womensrunning network.co.uk** have a comprehensive, area-by-area directory of women-only running groups.

> **Fact:** Self-awareness or self-protection classes are more advisable for runners than self-defence, as they concentrate less on fighting and more on avoiding a fight. You will probably still be taught a groin kick and an eye gouge, though.

Always report it

If you are attacked or dangerously harassed while out running, make sure you report it at the local police station. Even if the police can't do anything about your particular incident they might be more alert to what could occur in the future. Do your best to remember as much as you can about your assailant.

Tip: If it suits you to do your running in the evenings, look for a club to join so you can go out as part of a group.

Fact: Every distance runner is equipped with one highly effective weapon: larger-than-average lung capacity. A full-bodied scream should be enough to make most attackers think twice.

Tip: If you do get into any sort of confrontation, avoid getting angry – it's more important to stay in complete control of yourself.

It is not very probable that you'll be physically attacked while out running, but it is possible, and although women feel more vulnerable than men as regards actual assault, they are much less likely to get involved in anything physical. Whether it's because men are less worried about incidents and therefore less vigilant, or because men tend to be more confrontational when they believe they are under threat, Home Office statistics show that the vast proportion of violent incidents in the UK are committed by young men on other young men.

If faced with physical danger your first option should be to run away – after all, the chances are that you will be fitter and faster than your attacker. Try not to panic and run blindly; stick to your route (either onwards or back the way you came) because you'll know where you're going so it will give you one less thing to think about. Head to where you know there will be other people. If flight is not an immediate option, make as much noise as you can, which will either serve to put your assailant off completely or make him hesitate – either should give you the chance to run. See panel opposite for loud options.

If fighting back is absolutely unavoidable, carry on making noise – it will be very unnerving and will release your inner energy – and go for the groin or the eyes. Look on any blow you might land as a prelude to flight rather than fight. Think of it as one more distraction to allow you to get away, and once you've made your strike don't hang about. If it has stopped your attacker, you need to start running as quickly as possible; if it hasn't, you need to start running even quicker, because it's unlikely another blow would have any more effect.

Bring the noise

There are a number of hand-held personal alarms on the market, retailing at around £7 ($10) and they are worth their price if simply carrying one makes you feel safer when out running. They all function fairly well when it comes to quickly making a racket, and differences will be in how easy they are to carry and how swiftly you could get it to work. A wrist strap is a must, and remember to avoid tensing your arm when you carry it. However, effective as these are, several runners I know take the couple-of-quid option and run with a referee's whistle looped around one wrist.

Road safety

There are two important things to remember when running on the road: cars are faster than you and harder than you. Don't try to race one to a road junction or through a gap. It will beat you, the driver may get gladiatorial and if your adrenaline starts pumping your safety won't be uppermost in your mind. However, show cars and their drivers some respect and the chances are it will be reciprocated – it's rare that I go out for a run without at least one "after you… no, after you" scenario with a car at a corner. If there is no

Fact: Road safety for runners isn't that much different from road safety for pedestrians, except it all happens that bit faster.

Fact: Reflective clothing has become more prevalent as manufactures build shiny strips into a greater range of garments, but more than half the runners who regularly run after dark still don't own any.

pavement, run facing oncoming traffic, and if running after dark, makes sure you have reflective strips front and back – even if there is street lighting. Don't cross against traffic lights unless you are absolutely certain, as stopping will be furthest from any approaching driver's mind. Be aware of cars that you see parking ahead of you in case a door opens across the pavement, and don't be tempted to nip across a road from between parked cars. Watch out for cyclists, too, especially at junctions coming against the lights and going the wrong way up one-way streets.

Rural running

Just like urban environments, the countryside or larger open spaces in cities have their own set of dangers. Solitude is the biggest worry for runners, as there could be nobody within miles of your turned ankle or cracked head. Make sure you have a mobile phone with you if running by yourself in the countryside, and find out beforehand where there is and isn't coverage.

Cross-country running requires extra care regarding overhanging branches, exposed tree roots and rabbit holes, while brambles and stinging nettles also need to be avoided. If you do run through stinging nettles look for a dock leaf – broad flat leaves growing nearby – crush it and rub it on the affected area to relieve itching. The underside of a fern leaf will also do the job. Once you get home try not to scratch it, instead rub with ice.

Most deer you will come across will be pretty docile and will run away when they see you coming towards them. However, during rutting season (late autumn), stags will always be aggressive. Likewise deer with new foals (late spring) can respond viciously to even the slightest perceived threat to their young.

Right of way is a big deal in the countryside. Don't assume that just because a field is open you can run across it. If you are going cross-country, stick to acknowledged footpaths or make sure permission has been granted to access the land. If you're on accredited ramblers' routes, avoid any fields with animals in them – they might be fine for walkers but your running might agitate the occupants. The Ramblers Association, **www.ramblers.org.uk**, has plenty of information about rights of way.

Tip: If you are going to do a lot of running through woods it's worth making sure your running jacket is resistant to briars and brambles.

Fact: Steer clear of horses. Every time. They're psycho.

A load of bulls

The red rag to a bull theory is nonsense. It's the movement of the matador's cape the bull is charging at, not the fact that it is red. So a bull will come after you if you run past it regardless of what colours you are wearing.

Tip: To avoid interest from wasps or bees, don't wear bright colours or strong perfume or cologne as both will attract flying insects.

Storm warning

When running in the countryside always check the weather forecast and don't be a slave to your schedule; postpone your run if the weather is likely to turn as you won't have the same options for shelter as there would be in town. In fact, if you are going to do a great deal of rural running, you should invest in good waterproofs as it is so much easier to get to hypothermic levels of cold if you get soaked through because wet skin loses heat far more drastically.

You're more likely to get knocked down by a car or bitten by a dog than be struck by lightning, so although it can be scary if you're caught out in an electrical storm, you're probably pretty safe. You will need to take precautions, though. Head for cover as soon as you see the storm – it might be some way away but lightning can strike up to twenty miles from the storm itself. Don't shelter under a lone tree or isolated tall structure, and if in a wood take cover beneath small trees. Crouching in a hollow or gully is a good idea but only if it's dry – you don't want to get caught in a stream or standing water. Head for a building, or if in a car keep the windows closed.

If you are caught in the open, squat down and curl yourself into the tightest ball possible to present the smallest target. Balance on the balls of your feet as the less there is touching the ground, the less you're likely to absorb an electrical charge. If you are in a group that is caught out in a storm, do not huddle together but crouch into balls at least five metres apart.

> The biggest hazard I know is running in the snow past a school – any school. The kids will always regard you as a legitimate target for snowballs! They'll ignore people walking or cycling and carry on throwing snowballs at each other, but as soon as a runner comes round the corner…
> **Hugh Jones**

A doggy dog world

If you are bothered by a dog, don't try to outrun it – you won't succeed. Stand still until it gets bored and slopes off. If faced with one about to attack (head and shoulders lowered, and snarling), don't make any sudden movements and avoid making eye contact

– dogs take this as a threat. Keep watching it, talk to it in a steady voice, and back away slowly. The chances are that once it sees you are no threat to its territory it will relax. If you are bitten, go limp – don't thrash about or it will bite deeper to hang on. If the dog's owner cannot be found, report any dog bites to the police.

Watch out, there's a thief about!

Don't take any more with you than you have to when you go out running. If you drive to your run, don't leave valuables in your car – if you don't need them on the run why would you need them on the drive to and from? If you have to take stuff with you, don't leave it in the glove box, and doubly don't make a show of locking it in the boot, because you don't know who could be watching you run away from your car. Keep your house keys with you at all times.

Safe running dos and don'ts

✘ Don't run by yourself if you can avoid it.

✔ Carry coins for a phone call if you are leaving your mobile behind.

✔ Wear reflective clothing after dark, even in areas with street lights.

✘ Don't stop to give directions or the time or have any stationary contact with strangers.

✔ Run facing oncoming traffic.

✔ Carry identification, an emergency contact number and medical details.

✘ Don't run the same route at the same time each outing.

✔ Be alert to your surroundings.

✔ Keep your phone or mp3 player out of sight.

✘ Don't try to outrun a dog, or most other animals for that matter.

Injury time

It doesn't matter how careful you might be, running is a potentially hazardous activity.

It's not as risky as base jumping or black run skiing, obviously, but anything that involves pounding your entire body weight onto concrete, several hundred times an hour for a couple of hours at a time, is not going to be something your ankles, knees and hips were designed for. As a result, this section is one of the longest in the book as it looks at the most common runners' injuries, what causes them, how they can be avoided and how to treat them if they do occur.

What's likely to go wrong?

You will suffer some form of injury at some point during your running life. This is pretty much a given, as in any one year seventy per cent of all serious runners will pick up an injury severe enough to make them miss a week or more's running. And it can also be taken as read that this will be a pretty miserable time for you; as well as the discomfort of the injury itself, not running for however long it takes to get better will cast serious shadows on your usually sunny disposition. Which is why in this book we are putting so much stress on keeping you injury free.

On the up side, though, running injuries are seldom as traumatic as those received in a contact sport. Indeed, distance running's gentle, always-in-control way of doing things means that serious trauma is far more likely to be brought on by extraneous factors than by the physical demands of the activity itself – tripping over a dog, colliding with an overhanging branch, falling off a curb, that sort of thing. Although a degree of diligence on your part will minimize such incidents, no matter how careful you are there will always be events you can't legislate for. A runner I know was literally blown off her feet by a freak gust of wind on the River Thames embankment, and broke her arm in two places when she was slammed into a metal post. But she always was a special case.

Tip: There is evidence to show that 45 miles a week should be your upper limit – any more than that will not improve your performance or increase your stamina, but will considerably raise your chance of injury.

// I've had long spells out with injuries, but I've never stopped believing that I'm a runner – I'm either a runner or an injured runner. When I come back from an injury I know I've got to start a bit further back in the pack, and the numbers on the watch are a bit higher than they used to be, but I'm still there, competing against myself. //
Karen Hancock

It could be anything

Often a body part will get damaged and start hurting as a result of keeping the strain off some other apparently unrelated part, which is where the problem actually lies. I know a runner who thought he had back problems, and after seeing several specialists discovered he had a problem with his ankle and the incorrect technique he had adopted to keep his weight off it as he ran had been twisting his back.

Furthermore, because of the self-contained nature of running, the vast majority of running injuries are self-inflicted, therefore entirely avoidable and usually self-treatable. Indeed, most running injures occur for one or more of these four reasons: over-use, lack of preparation, unsuitable equipment or poor technique. They will mostly involve damage to soft tissue (muscles and tendons) rather than hard tissue (bones and cartilage), and so will rarely come as a surprise but will be the result of a build-up of tissue stress or neglect over a period of time.

Even injuries caused by failing to warm up properly will be progressive, albeit over a much shorter period of time. Consequently, running injuries are *caused* rather than *happen*, and as such are largely preventable. Also, the chronic nature of so many of them means they will provide warning signs so vivid it will often be more trouble to ignore them than to pay them attention.

After examining the main causes of runners' injuries and some of the key ways of preventing and treating them, in the Lexicon of hurt (p.160) we'll look at specific ailments and how to treat them.

Bad shoes

If you are suffering unexplained and repetitive pains, wherever they are on your body, check your shoes first!

In the Running gear section (see pp.42–51), we devoted a great deal of space to the importance of choosing the right running shoes. This is because the wrong shoes or a badly fitting pair can have adverse effects far beyond your feet. Yet running on shoes that are not right for you or are worn out is widespread. As every running club, shop or magazine will confirm, both prospective and experienced runners *have* to buy shoes from a specialist running shop rather than a general sports store for them to be fitted correctly.

> // You should always keep a training diary, but it's very important to do so when you're coming back from an injury because you need to be sure of what you are doing and how it feels so you don't push yourself too far. //
> **Karen Hancock**

Doctor! Doctor!

Much as I advised it probably wouldn't be necessary to get checked out by your doctor before you start running, don't make a trip to the surgery unless an injury persists for too long after you have taken your own action – see R.I.C.E. (p.156). Then, if you have to seek medical attention, make sure you see a doctor with experience in athletes' injuries, otherwise the chances are you'll simply be told "Don't go running for a couple of weeks and see if it clears up".

Ill-fitting shoes will either rub or pinch or both, and so often it's relatively little niggles such as blisters or bruising, rather than serious damage, that can mean the difference between finishing a race or dropping out. Shoes that don't provide enough support for your size or type of running will leave you particularly vulnerable to ankle injuries. However, shoes that are wrong for your particular pronation can lead to serious damage – instead of countering aspects of the stride, incorrect shoes will overstate them, putting unwarranted strain on the lower leg and increasing the chance of ankle or knee injury.

Don't run on the same pair of shoes for longer than 500 miles or six months – less if you are above average weight

A supinator (whose lower leg rolls outwards) wearing shoes designed for an over-pronator (rolls inwards) will have their lower leg pushed even further out from vertical, while in the opposite situation the leg will be pushed too far inwards. In each case, the knee joint will be forced to take the body's weight at an awkward angle, and in turn push the ankle out of line. This can often manifest itself in apparently unexplained hip or lower back pains, as the body tries to compensate higher up. It will also affect your performance, as not lining the lower leg up properly will waste a huge amount of energy generated from elastic recoil.

Worn-out shoes probably claim far more victims than the wrong shoes, as it is so easy to carry on for a few more months with a pair of shoes that "seem alright". But if the midsole has collapsed, the shoes will no longer be providing the cushioning they should do, and the impact as each step hits the concrete will be transmitted, virtually undampened, to ankle, knee and hip joints, resulting in internal inflammation such as bursitis. This lack of shock absorption puts you at enormous risk of stress fractures in the ankles and feet, particularly in the fragile metatarsals.

Sprains and strains

A sprain is a stretch or a tear in the connective tissue (ligaments) that joins one bone to another inside a joint. Because of the poorer blood supply in ligaments, a sprain usually takes longer to heal.

A strain is a stretch or a tear of a muscle or the tendons that connects it to the body.

Top five injuries at a glance

A bite-sized guide to what's most likely to befall you and how best to treat it and prevent it.

Injury	Cause	Remedy
Runner's knee Sharp pain under or just outside the knee cap	Weak quads; too much downhill running; over-pronation	Ice; cut down on mileage; check your shoes; build up quads
Shin splints Tearing pain down the muscles at the front of the legs	Weak muscles at the front of leg	Ice; cut down on mileage and build back up gently; run on softer surfaces
Achilles tendonitis Dull ache just above the heel	Tight calf muscles	Stretch Achilles tendons; cut down hill running; change to more flexible shoes
Black toenail One toenail, usually on the longest toe, turns black	Blood pooling under a toenail that has come loose or is being pressed into the toe by your shoe	It usually falls off by itself; if it comes back repeatedly get better-fitting running shoes
Iliotibial band syndrome Ache on the outside of the leg by the knee	Iliotibial band too tight to accommodate your stride's range of movement	Iliotibial band stretching; run on even ground

Fact: Even if you are just out for a gentle training run, warm up first. Although you can gradually increase the intensity of your cardiovascular rate as you run, to best protect yourself against injury you'll still need to achieve a certain level of joint mobility before you start running with any seriousness.

Tip: Don't allow yourself to cool down again after you have warmed up. Warming up too long before the start of a race, or standing around chatting when you should be dynamic stretching, can negate the warm-up as your cardiovascular rates will fall and the loosened tissue will contract once more.

Shoes with stretched uppers can allow more movement of the foot than is good for it, meaning that blisters and black toenails will be common injuries.

The wear on the outsoles of your shoes will show how you are putting your foot down as you run, and as that wear progresses, whatever aspect of your gait is causing it will be less controlled. Excessive wear on the inside or outside can undo the shoe's inherent corrective measures for over-pronating or supinating respectively, or make it considerably worse if the shoe was not compensating in the first place. If you are a heavy heel-striker, heel wear will mean a particularly sensitive part of your foot is now being given far less protection. This in itself can increase your chances of plantar fascitis and Achilles tendonitis, and, with your foot having to travel further to make contact with the ground, a worn-away heel can put strain on your calf muscles.

II If you're coming back at the correct pace, not rushing, it will take you roughly twice as long as you were out injured to regain your pre-injury levels. So if you were out for a month it'll take about two to get back to where you were.
Karen Hancock *II*

How bad could it be?

A degree of discomfort as you cover long distances is to be expected, but there are steps along the road to "potentially dangerous" that you need to be aware of.

Aching muscles an hour or so after your run or when you get up the next morning are nothing to worry about.

Aches during your run that do not get progressively worse as you continue will be alright to run with but should be attended to later at home.

Sudden, sharp pains during your run that prohibit your usual running action mean you should stop. If they go away when you stop, start again slowly – heading towards home. If they return, pack up for the day, if not carry on.

A progressive pain – progressive as you run and from run to run – means you should stop before it stops you.

Failure to warm up properly

The best way to think about running without warming up properly is to compare it to starting a car that has been standing overnight, then, as soon as the engine catches, flooring the accelerator. Internal parts would be grating against each other as the oil pressure struggled to raise itself, and parts and openings not yet expanded wouldn't be able to cope with this sort of thrashing. You might get away with it once or twice, but to do it all the time would drastically shorten the car's life.

Running without warming up is one of the primary causes of tissue sprains and strains, and can lead to internal joint damage like bursitis or synovial cavity inflammation. As previously discussed, elevating the cardiovascular rate pumps blood faster to deliver higher volumes of oxygen to the muscles, and to facilitate this the blood vessels have to dilate. This is vital to avoid injury, as it lowers the muscle's viscosity, increasing the elasticity and extensibility of the internal fibres, without which they would be far more susceptible to strain.

A cold system is liable to bursitis or internal joint bruising. By raising your body's operating levels you will increase the flow of synovial fluid – the thick fluid that lubricates the parts of the joints that come into contact with each other – making the joint move much more smoothly. This rise in internal temperature will also decrease the stickiness of the synovial fluid in the sacs that sit between the muscles or tendons and the bones, meaning they provide more comfortable cushioning as the soft and hard tissues move across each other.

Dynamic stretching (see pp.84–85) as part of your warm-up before intense exercise will go a long way towards preventing sprained ankles or knees. A dynamic stretching routine gently eases out

Joint maintenance

As a runner, your joints will be under constant unnatural stress, and require a constant supply of blood to regenerate damaged tissue. For this reason ensuring a healthy circulation can contribute enormously to preventing and relieving the joint pains all runners will suffer. A supplement such as cod liver oil can be vital too, as you will need a higher-than-average intake of omega-3 fatty acids to work against the body's production of prostaglandins and leukotrienes, the chief contributors to joint inflammation. Taking glucosamine sulphate and chrondroitin sulphate (usually found in the same tablet) can help speed up the repair of damaged cartilage.

the ligaments that connect one bone to another inside a joint, elongating the tissue and loosening it to reduce internal resistance. This means that when it comes under stress as you run, it can absorb the new demands rather than be forced to stretch or tear.

Poor technique

When you consider that *Homo sapiens* were never originally designed to walk without the aid of their knuckles, let alone run – upright! – for 26.2 miles, it's obvious that *how* we do it will be very important. Correct running technique is covered in Big steps forward (see pp.92–105), but what happens if you continue without good technique over a long period definitely belongs here in Injury time. In fact, running badly is the cause of nearly as many cumulative injuries as knackered shoes, and very often it is hard to pin down because where you hurt might be nowhere near the aspect of your stride that is going wrong.

Most commonly, bad technique will involve too much up-and-down instead of forward movement. This breaks one of the golden rules of running: don't stop a movement, redirect it. High striding is a common beginner's mistake – pushing off upwards with the toes – and as what goes up has to come down, this means stopping the movement by landing hard on to the pavement. Each stride sends a shockwave through your body, jolting joints in ways that can cause internal damage and inviting stress fractures of the feet. Pushing off with the toes also increases the risk of hamstring strains – rare in distance runners – because the action will tense the quads meaning the hamstrings have to work much harder to provide their push.

Over-striding is another danger, especially going down hills (see pp.104–105). If your feet land a long way in front of your body, the movement involved in "catching up" (bringing your body directly over where you are making contact with the ground) will

Check the technique

The rule of thumb is, if you have a pain that is only there when you are running and it gets worse the longer you run it's a technique problem. (Bear in mind, though, that worn-out shoes may also be throwing your mechanics off.) Examine your technique and make adjustments to iron out the discomfort. Then, once you start covering long distances with this new style, only run as far as you can without slipping back into your old ways. As soon as you find yourself doing this, stop for the day. Because, until running in a different style etches itself onto your muscle memory, you will have to concentrate on it, you will tire more quickly than normal and once you do you will slip back into your old harmful ways.

put undue stress on your knee joints and, to a lesser degree, your ankles. Heel runners will always be more liable to shin splints and Achilles tendonitis. However, if repeatedly pounded in this manner, your heels could also suffer stress fractures. Those landing heavily on the ball of the foot will be putting strain on their Achilles tendon as it will naturally contract to absorb the strike.

Aside from these specific points, there is virtually no limit to the amount of pain that can be caused by poor running technique. Correct running styles are there to utilize the laws of nature and gravity and keep us moving forward with a minimum of tension, impact or joint stress. Problems caused by poor technique will usually give you plenty of warning before something serious occurs, so be aware of any pains that continually happen while you are on the road.

Overtraining

This is pretty self-explanatory and will be very common among new runners as the temptation to "get stuck in" will be enormous. Overtraining will bring its own particular set of discomforts

> Runners coming back from injuries often feel demoralized because they think they'll be going back to square one and so they put off getting out there again, which only makes those feelings worse. Sure, you will have lost stamina and you will have lost speed, but you won't be back at square one. More like square three or four, and if you understand the theories of training you know you'll be back. You won't get any fitter by not running.
> **Karen Hancock**

injury time

> Often other people will see the signs of your overtraining before you do – tiredness, drastic weight loss, loss of appetite, aching joints – you might think you're just working out hard and getting fitter. Listen to other people if they comment on how you seem.
>
> **Efua Baker**

– nausea, muscle stiffness within a few hours, muscle soreness the next day, exhaustion, shin splints and knee problems in the long term – and they will apply to experienced runners as well as beginners. Equally worryingly, overtraining will aggravate and make worse any other niggles you might have (see box below) and without doubt it is the most reliable way to turn minor injuries into serious injuries.

There are simple rules to remember as regards overtraining. Don't run through the pain barrier – you'll experience some mild discomfort during and after training but any serious pain is telling you to stop. Don't overdo it – pretty obvious, but surprisingly neglected. If you are a novice, go with a programme such as the one on p.19, or if building up to a long race run, follow the ten per cent guideline – don't bump up your mileage by more than that amount per week. Allow your body to recover by taking plenty of rest days, and alternate tough and easy training days.

Over-use injuries

This is the term for any injury that has occurred over time, as a result of some chronic condition. It includes much of the above, as it refers to any problem that has been allowed to persist or a condition/body part that has been repeatedly abused – this could be the result of bad shoes, bad technique or regularly running past your natural limits. Over-use injuries can be serious, but will always be flagged up by severe and perpetual discomfort. They are proof that the "No pain, no gain" maxim, when applied to distance running, is nonsense.

Ice is the answer

After shoes, ice is probably a runner's best friend. Some runners I know go as far as dousing their legs in ice water every time they come in from a long run. Personally, as a runner's knee sufferer,

I ice up my left knee for about ten minutes as soon as I get home. An ice pack will usually be the first thing prescribed for any over-training injury.

If soft tissue or a joint has become inflamed – and most knees and rear leg muscles will after 10k, even if they don't hurt at the time – massaging it with ice will greatly speed recovery. The blood vessels below the skin have been damaged and have expanded to allow a greater flow of disorganised blood cells into the tissue, breaking it down – this is what causes swelling, discolouration and pain. Icing the area shrinks these blood vessels down, allowing much less blood through and arresting tissue damage as this slows the metabolic process. The swelling will be reduced, the pain will be much less and the healing process will be speeded up.

Gel-filled ice packs and bags of frozen peas are alright, but they tend to warm up too quickly, reducing their effectiveness. The best thing to use is an ice cup – a regular paper cup filled with water and frozen. When you need an ice pack, simply take it from the freezer, hold it by the cup and massage the ice top across the affected area. As it melts while you use it, tear the paper away in a spiral to expose more ice, then put it back in the freezer for the next time. It is more effective than a standard ice pack because as the water melts it can get to every contour of the injured area, which will remain very cold through contact with a block of ice.

> To properly understand the importance of ice to a runner, look no further than the example of Ed Moses, the legendary Olympic champion and world record holder for 400m hurdles. After every training session he would stand in a wheelie bin of ice. The rationale for this is that it reduces swelling and the microscopic bleeding from stressed capillaries. This would enable him to train again the following day, or do another session on the same day. Maybe most runners don't need to go to those lengths, but icing up is well worth doing after a run if only to target a suspect joint such as a knee or ankle.
> **Barrie Savory D.O.**

Fact: Don't apply heat to running injuries. Although it might appear to soothe any aches and pains, it will be having exactly the opposite effect to ice and therefore will be making them worse.

R.I.C.E.

Like penicillin or chicken soup in other circumstances, R.I.C.E. is pretty much a universal runners' remedy. It is a cure for sprains, strains, bursitis or internal bruising, which make up the majority of minor running injuries.

Rest: Don't try to run off an injury. Take a few days' rest and try to keep weight off the affected area as much as possible.

Ice: Putting ice on an injury, no matter how small, will do wonders to ease it by reducing internal swelling and numbing any pain.

Compression: A tightly applied bandage, athletic support or elastic wrap will reduce swelling in a joint, help immobilize it and keep it stable if weight has to be applied.

Elevation: Raising the injured area – preferably above the level of the heart – will stop blood pooling there and so reduce swelling and discomfort.

Strengthening strategies

A high level of core strength will contribute enormously to a distance runner's injury protection programme for several reasons. Well-developed muscles in the trunk – waist, lower back and hips – do much to absorb and dissipate the shockwaves transmitted up from impact with the road. These same areas, and the upper body, will then provide more stable pivots for the legs and arms, reducing the likelihood of their movement straying off line. The stronger you are generally, the better you'll cope with the rigours of running, as increased muscle strength minimizes inherent joint stress as the muscles will assume more of the load from connective tissue and bones – in the case of the kneecap, you'll need strong quadricep muscles to hold it in place. Strength training will also strengthen ligaments and tendons as it works the muscles.

Importantly, working certain specific muscles provides the muscle balance necessary to reduce the risk of straining the muscles that have to work hard. For example, runners' hamstrings are agonist muscles (directly causing movement) and will naturally develop out of proportion to the quads which are antagonist (they slow, stop or control that movement), yet if the quads are not strong enough, added strain will be placed on the hamstrings to control themselves. See pp.126–129 for a programme of running-specific strength exercises.

Drug-free zone

Contrary to many running books and guides, we do not encourage the use of pain killers when recovering from an injury. In fact, we strongly discourage it. Quite apart from the fact that pharmaceutical pain killers are dangerously addictive drugs, pain is there for a reason – to tell you something is wrong with your body that has to be fixed or rested. To deaden that pain in order to continue running would be like putting a gag on a doctor who is trying to give you free medical advice. Professional sport has a living legacy of nearly-crippled middle-aged ex-athletes who were dosed up with pain killers in order to keep them in the game – don't join them.

Natural advantages

To give yourself that edge, there are a number of natural supplements you can take to reduce the likelihood of injury and to boost your recovery.

Supplement	What it is	What it does	How it is taken
Arnica	Extract of the flower of the arnica plant (also called leopard's bane)	Reduces bruise swelling by removing congested blood; promotes wound healing by stimulating activity of white blood cells; fights bacterial infection; soothes chapped lips	As balm, rubbed on to affected area; or as tiny tablets
Bicarbonate of soda	Baking soda	The alkali, usually used to neutralize stomach acid, also protects against acid build-up in the muscles of endurance athletes	Dissolved in water
Boswellia	Extracted from the gum of the boswellia tree – commonly known as frankincense	Combats joint pain and bruising; the acids in boswellia increase circulation in damaged tissue and reduce swelling by dispersing congested blood	Capsules
Chromium	Mineral found in broccoli and grapefruit	Helps insulin to process carbohydrate, building and maintaining muscle, burning fat and producing energy more efficiently	Capsules
Cod liver oil	Oil from cods' livers, the most effective source of omega-3 fatty acid	Combats joint damage by reducing prostaglandins and leukotrienes that contribute to internal wear and cause inflammation – very important for older runners. Helps keep the heart healthy	Capsules

Ginseng	Extracted from the root of the panax plant	During endurance tests ginseng has been shown to boost VO_2 max and reduce heart rate and oxygen consumption, but it has as many detractors as runners who swear by it as an energy supplement	Tablets
Glucosamine	An amino sugar naturally produced within the body	Counteracts degenerative joint damage by stimulating production of cartilage's chief ingredients	Tablets
Magnesium	Mineral making up one per cent of the Earth's crust, found in spinach, nuts and whole grains	Helps prevents muscle cramps, as it is the most important electrolyte without which the others such as potassium and calcium cannot get absorbed into the muscles	Tablets
Vitamin C	An essential nutrient, found in fruit and green veg	Repairs damaged or worn cartilage by aiding the production of collagen, and, as an antioxidant, protects the joints from the molecules that cause inflammation when the joint is put under stress	Dissolved in water
Vitamin E	Tocopherol, an important antioxidant, found in oils and nuts	Protects against muscle soreness by inhibiting the activity of free radicals within the muscles	Capsules
Zinc	An essential element	Speeds recovery by aiding tissue repair and increasing blood cell production; boosts immune systems left depleted by long runs	Tablets or lozenges

The lexicon of hurt

Your A–Z of the aches and pains associated with running, starting from the ground up and detailing preventions as well as cures.

Feet

Because the average runner's foot hits the ground around five hundred times per kilometre, each time absorbing an impact equivalent to three times that runner's weight, feet are the most likely point of injury. Indeed, so many running injuries start in the feet but manifest themselves somewhere else in the running action as incorrect foot placement throws your delicately balanced biomechanics out of line. This is shown in the sheer number of running injuries described that list over-pronation – the foot

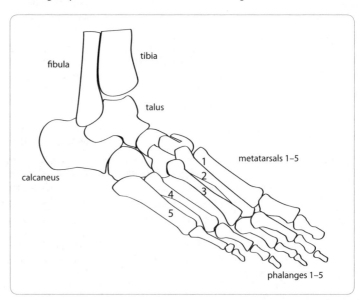

rolling too far inwards as it hits the ground – among their causes. It is why so much emphasis is put on runners getting fitted for the right shoes and replacing them as soon as they start to wear out.

Another reason to make sure you're not running on collapsed shoes is the shock absorption. The fully developed human foot contains 26 separate bones, 19 muscles and 107 ligaments, so it's a very fragile mechanism in its own right and stress fractures and bruising are very common occurrences. Also, as the shoes need to prevent impact being transmitted up the legs to the shins, knees and hips, there is even more potential for injury originating in the feet.

> *Everybody should try a pair of orthotics (custom-moulded insoles for your shoes), even if they're not suffering from pains or injuries. They're like having your shoes tailor-made, and will support your feet so completely that all your muscles and joints will function correctly.*
> **Efua Baker**

Athlete's foot
Fungal infections in the skin of the feet are not merely the preserve of athletes.
Symptoms: Cracking and splitting of the skin, usually underneath and between the toes. If it goes deep enough it can leave painful raw tissue exposed.
Causes: This infection can come from other people – damp changing rooms are notorious – and you can pick it up from micro-organisms in the soil or even from animals.
Self-help: There are a number of anti-fungal creams, paints and sprays available over the counter. Air your feet by going barefoot as much as possible.
Prevention: Athlete's foot thrives in the damp, so make sure you dry your feet thoroughly – especially between and under your toes. Dust your feet with talc before putting fresh socks on. Also, make sure your shoes (running shoes and everyday shoes) have dried out completely before you put them on over clean socks.

Black toenail
A blood blister between the toenail and the nail bed.
Symptoms: Er, a toenail turns black. It usually affects the nail on your longest toe.

Tip: To sterilize a needle, submerse it in boiling water or hold it in a flame for a few seconds. Let it cool in the air before using it – don't put it down on any surface or that will re-contaminate it.

Causes: Your toe banging against the inside of the toebox of the shoe, either because it doesn't fit properly, because of a longer-than-usual-run (a marathon?), or a great deal of running down hills.

Self-help: Black toenails rarely hurt, and usually fall off by themselves. To get rid of a black toenail push a sterile needle through it, drain the blood, apply antiseptic and a dressing.

Prevention: Better-fitting shoes.

Blisters

Formed as a defence against friction or traction, they are usually found on the soles or sides of the feet.

Symptoms: Fluid collecting in a "bubble" under an area of separated skin in order to protect a part of the foot that is rubbing.

Causes: Ill-fitting shoes or sweat creating an abrasive effect.

Self-help: Most blisters burst of their own accord and give no more trouble. If you need to pop one, use a sterile needle, mop the fluid up immediately and dress the wound. Do not remove the dead skin as this will be protecting a very tender layer of new skin.

Prevention: Make sure your shoes fit and keep your feet dry with talcum powder. If you start to notice friction building up on a long run, alleviate it using Vaseline.

Hard skin

Thickening of the skin (hyperkeratosis) on the heels and balls of feet, causing calluses as the layers of skin build up on top of each other to protect an area that is under stress.

Symptoms: Affected areas are painful under pressure and shoes no longer fit properly.

Causes: Running for long periods of time can naturally cause a build-up of hard skin – marathon runners are particularly prone to it – as can ill-fitting running shoes. Once calluses start to form, they will continue to grow as further pressure will be added by the layers of dead skin as they build up.

Self-help: Hard skin should be removed with foot shavers or pumice stones, then moisturizing cream applied.

Prevention: Runners should moisturize their feet two or three times a week and remove any hard skin as soon as it appears.

Metatarsal fractures

See Stress fractures, p.164.

Mid-foot pain

Symptoms: Pain in the middle of the sole of the foot, usually linked to the stride and not present while resting.

Causes: Stress fracture of the mid-tarsal, a complex joint that connects the metatarsals to the top of the ankle; strain on the tendons that pull the toes upwards; supination, as the foot is losing cushioning ability because it isn't rolling far enough inwards; arch strain – if you have an exceptionally high foot arch that isn't being properly supported it can cause pain as stride impact and gravity mean it starts to collapse.

Self-help: R.I.C.E. or, for stress fractures, see p.164.

Prevention: Correct or simply better-cushioned shoes will support the foot properly to guard against supination or impact damage, while an orthotic insert or brace will support a high arch. Inflammation of the tendons along the top of the foot can often be eased by not tying shoe laces quite so tight.

Plantar fascitis

Inflammation of the plantar fascia, the wishbone-shaped strip of connective tissue that runs from the heel down each side of the foot to the ball.

Symptoms: Pain running down the bottom of the foot, from the heel to the arch, often worse first thing in the morning or after sitting or standing still for a long time.

Causes: As a runner lands on their heel, the plantar fascia, a thick ligament that cannot move too much, absorbs and transmits the impact with its limited flexibility – the damage occurs when it is forced to move too far. This happens because the calf muscle or

Tip: If you are experiencing mid-foot pain or you are coming back from stress fractures, it is vital that you switch to a soft surface.

Achilles tendon is too tight and the plantar fascia is trying to flex to compensate, or because the shoes are too rigid and the ligament is straining against them. Over-pronators who are not wearing the correct motion-control shoes or anybody in worn-out shoes will be particularly vulnerable, as will runners with high foot arches because in each case the plantar fascia is forced to work harder.

Self-help: This soreness eases out with activity, so it is okay to run on it. Altering your stride to alleviate any pain is not a good idea, though. Icing the soles of the feet will treat any immediate pain while flexing and massaging will loosen the plantar fascia.

Prevention: The correct shoes, combined with well-stretched calves and Achilles tendons, are the best prevention.

Stress fractures

Tiny cracks in and minute fragmentation of bones – metatarsal bones and shins are particularly susceptible.

Symptoms: Chronic pain, increasing as you run and causing swelling. Even when it isn't actually hurting, an affected area will be very tender to touch.

Causes: Towards the end of a long run, when muscles get tired and can't provide enough shock absorption, the bones in your feet and lower legs will have to assume too much of each stride's impact. Worn-out shoes can also lead to stress fractures. As an over-use injury, they can be brought on by sudden increases in distance or attempting to run too far too soon.

Self-help: It is important that stress fractures heal completely, so this means no running and plenty of R.I.C.E. for between four weeks and four months, depending on the severity of the injury.

Prevention: Make sure your shoes are still providing cushioning, increase your distances gradually and, because stress fractures are progressive, always allow recovery days between runs.

Ankles and lower legs

Articulating the foot and lower leg as it lands and pushes off each stride, the ankle absorbs a huge amount of impact, yet is sufficiently stable and well constructed to cope. Under normal circumstances, that is. The most common runners' ankle injuries are sprains, strains and breaks resulting from extraordinary stress. The Achilles tendon is particularly vulnerable to both traumatic and over-use injuries, so it should not be neglected. Straining or tearing are the most frequent lower leg injuries, so make sure ankles are adequately warmed up and stretched to avoid excess tension while on the move.

Achilles tendonitis
Inflammation of the thick tendon that connects the heel to the muscles of the lower leg.
Symptoms: Pain and swelling in the Achilles tendon.
Causes: An over-use injury brought on by insufficient flexibility in the tendon to achieve the range of movement required – older

> **Fact:** The reason running shoes have the v-shaped cut at the heel is to relieve any pressure on the Achilles tendon which could result in irritation and inflammation.

> **"** Apart from slips and falls, most runners' joint injuries are due to faulty mechanics, which ought to be put right as a matter of course rather than as a reaction to injury. Think of how badly the front tyres of a car would wear if the wheels were toed in at the wrong angle. It is no good putting on new tyres until you have corrected the front geometry. We are just the same – a fault in the mechanical function of one unit will affect another, which under the stress of the repetitive motion of running will lead to an injury. Runners should get checked out all over and not just the bits that are hurting at the time. **Barrie Savory D.O. "**

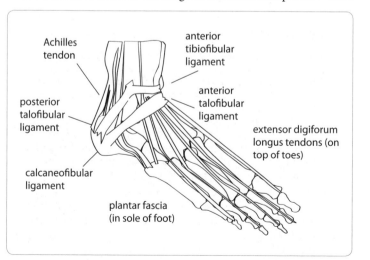

- Achilles tendon
- anterior tibiofibular ligament
- anterior talofibular ligament
- posterior talofibular ligament
- extensor digiforum longus tendons (on top of toes)
- calcaneofibular ligament
- plantar fascia (in sole of foot)

Tip: Shoes with too-soft heels – air- or gel-filled – can cause Achilles tendon strain as when the foot strikes the heel will drop to a level slightly below the rest of the sole.

> There is a great fallacy that 'everyone has one leg shorter than the other', with the implication that this is normal. It is not normal and is usually due to our habit of standing more on one leg than another. This forces the large wedge-shaped bone at the base of the spine – the sacrum – to lock, like a drawer stuck sideways in its runners. It produces the pelvic imbalance that results in the appearance of unequal leg length – this is one of the prices we human beings pay for standing upright.
> **Barrie Savory D.O.**

Fact: Bad sprains can hurt for months after the event, as the scar tissue that forms on the healthy tissue as it heals slightly increases it in size and can cause irritation.

runners whose tissue is less elastic will be more susceptible to this injury. It can also be brought on by tight calf muscles, overly rigid shoes or over-pronation. The injury will be exacerbated by sudden increases in distance or in the amount of hills you are running.

Self-help: Ice and rest. It is very important not to continue your regular running regime until the swelling has gone down – it will be noticeable – as the microscopic tears in the tendon that have caused the swelling can easily progress into a full-blown rupture.

Prevention: Make sure Achilles tendons and calf muscles are well stretched; avoid sudden increases in mileage or hill running; and if your shoes have no give in them from front to back opt for a more flexible pair.

Ankle sprain

The stretching or tearing of one of the ligaments that connect the ankle's three bones.

Symptoms: Sharp pain and continued ache, then swelling in the affected part of the joint.

Check out those legs

Apparently 32 per cent of us have a leg length discrepancy – that is, one leg more than half an inch shorter than the other. Most will go through life without even realising they've got it, by compensating in their walking gait. But if you're putting in mega miles each week it will take its toll, especially if you start tiring, and can manifest itself in iliotibial band syndrome, piriformis syndrome, lower back pain or hip pain. While each of those symptoms should be treated as suggested in their individual entries, you should counter a leg length discrepancy with orthotics, either as a heel lift or a full sole in one shoe. A running shop or sports physiotherapist should be able to advise you.

To find out if you've got it, stand in front of a full-length mirror, shake yourself out and loosely jump up and down to totally relax, then look to see if one shoulder is lower than the other. If it is, that's how much shorter that leg is.

Causes: Sudden twisting of the ankle caused by stepping awkwardly on a very uneven surface such as the edge of a hole, the curb or a raised tree root, which forces the joint to move unnaturally and sharply, damaging the internal connective tissue.

Self-help: R.I.C.E. Immediately. And no running for at least two weeks. Try to keep off the ankle completely as much as possible during that time. After a fortnight, the swelling should be going down and the pain decreasing.

Prevention: The sort of accident that can sprain an ankle is so random that it cannot really be protected against. If you are prone to sprained ankles, though, avoid running on uneven surfaces, buy running shoes that offer more support or stability, and make sure your ankles are stretched before and after a run.

Calf strain

Tearing of the calf muscle – this can range from micro-tearing as a result of stretching, to full-on rupture.

Symptoms: The micro-tearing will give a increasing dull ache in the calf, progressing both as you run and run by run, as unhealed tears slowly get bigger. The more severe rupture will cause a sharp stabbing pain and a noticeable "pop". This "pop" is similar to an Achilles tendon tear, but in all cases of calf strain the pain will be higher up the leg than the Achilles.

Causes: Over exertion of a too-tight calf muscle, particularly the sudden acceleration or a dramatic increase in hill running; shoes that allow the heel to drop below the level of the rest of the sole; over-pronation putting increased stress on the lower leg.

Self-help: R.I.C.E., and take a break from running until it no longer gives you any pain – this could be between two weeks and two months depending on the severity of the strain. Before returning to running, carefully go through a programme of static and dynamic calf stretching and strengthening exercises. Calf strains rarely require surgery, but if pain persists after several weeks, seek medical advice.

Tip: An ankle sprain might not hurt immediately. If you twist the joint badly enough for you to assume you might have done some damage, stop running and don't put any weight on it. If it doesn't start hurting in thirty seconds or so it's alright and you can continue. If it does, then you have a sprain and even running a few more steps on it could make the damage much worse.

Prevention: Thorough stretching and warming up of the calves before you set off; the correct shoes.

Shin splints

Medial tibial stress syndrome, a pretty general term given to problems in the front of the leg between knee and ankle. It can be related to the muscles, the bones or the tendons joining them together.

Symptoms: Aches and pains running down the shins.

Causes: Very common over-use injury for new runners, as the activity will not develop the front and inside of the leg as fast it develops the calf muscles, therefore the medial muscles and tendons (those at the front and inside) become overworked. This results in strain on the muscles and can start to microscopically tear the tendon away from the shin bone. Without the muscle support, there will be undue stress on the shin bone itself, which can lead, in extreme cases, to stress fractures. Over-pronation can also contribute to shin splints as the foot's inward roll will put added strain on the muscles at the front of the shin.

Self-help: Ice will ease any immediate pain.

Prevention: New runners should cut back on duration and build back up slowly, allowing time for medial muscles to catch up with the others. Running on softer surfaces will help, as shin splint sufferers need to be fairly well developed as a runner to cope with the stress factor of road work. The correct shoes are also a must.

Knees

The knee is probably the most complex and fragile joint in the body, comprising two separate articulators, eight main ligaments and two cartilages. For a runner it is probably the most vulnerable joint as it regularly has to support the entire weight of the body while going through intricate ranges of motion. Cumulative stress injuries, sudden trauma, twisting, over extension... the knee is

> *II* The most common places for knee problems to originate are the pelvis and the foot. The problem in the foot is usually over-pronation, effectively a flat foot. This is very easily corrected in most good running shoes, but better addressed with a visit to a podiatrist, who can tailor-make corrective insoles – orthotics. The pelvis, with usually one leg shorter than the other, is equally easily remedied. This requires a capable osteopath or chiropractor to adjust and level out its two sides.
> **Barrie Savory D.O.** *II*

particularly prone to all of these, resulting in damage to ligaments or cartilage and a long delay before you run again. Look after your knees and they will look after you.

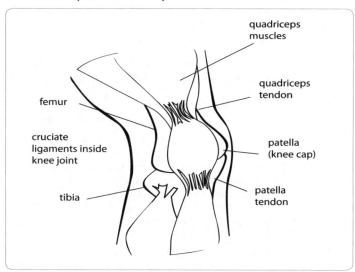

Bursitis

The swelling of bursae, the sacs of synovial fluid that lubricate the movement of tissue and bone against bone and cartilage. Although it can occur in any joint, it is, understandably, most common in runners' knees.

Symptoms: Pain and stiffness within joints, particularly bad first thing in the morning or after sitting still for a long time.

Causes: Jolting of or impact on the joints, or repetitive movement over a long period of time.

Self-help: R.I.C.E.

Prevention: Develop a smoother running style and make sure your shoes are adequately cushioned, or switch to a softer surface.

Who does what?

Osteopath: treats a body's damaged mechanical components – muscles, ligaments, joints and nerves. Restores balance to a body that may have become stressed or out of sync due to sporting injuries, RSI or posture-related problems. Everybody should visit an osteopath twice a year, more frequently when over the age of forty. Persistent or unexplained running pains should be taken to an osteopath who has experience with sporting injuries. Osteopaths in the UK are regulated by the General Osteopathic Council (**WWW. osteopathy.org.uk**). In the US, they are called osteopathic physicians, are licensed doctors and can carry out surgery or prescribe drugs.

Chiropractor: treats disorders of the spine and the muscularskeletal system. A complementary practice based on the notion that many of the body's ills originate through spinal disorders interfering with the nervous system, although the pain might manifest itself elsewhere. See a chiropractor if you get no joy from an osteopath. The Federation of Chiropractic Licensing Boards is the organization that coordinates chiropractic regulatory bodies around the world. **www.ability.org.uk/chiropractic_organizations**

Physiotherapist: carries out physical therapy on moving parts of the body, to ensure maximum, efficient and pain-free movement. This can include exercises, mobilization technique, manual therapy, manipulation and strengthening, treating damaged joints or strained or bruised soft tissue. Visits to physiotherapists are usually referrals from the above or your GP. In the UK, the profession is regulated by the Chartered Society of Physiotherapy (**www.csp.org.uk**). In the US, physiotherapists have to be licensed by whatever state they are practising in.

Collateral ligament injury

Rupture or stretching of one of the two ligaments that are either side of the knee joint – the medial collateral ligament (inside the knee) and the lateral (outside).

Symptoms: Immediate pain and swelling on whichever side of the knee the tissue has been damaged.

Causes: These ligaments prevent the knee moving too far inwards or outwards. Sudden pressure in either direction – stepping lengthways on the edge of a curb – will cause the damage.

Self-help: Stop running straight away – to carry on will make the injury worse. Apply R.I.C.E. These ligaments are much stronger than the cruciate ligaments (see below) and they play a big part in protecting them, thus collateral ligaments are much more likely to be stretched rather than ruptured. In which case, a couple of weeks' rest and initial frequent icings should sort it out.

Prevention: Strong quads will take much of the strain off these ligaments as they will do much to keep the leg straight as you run.

Cruciate ligament injury

The rupture or stretching of one of the two ligaments that sit in the knee joint between the shin bone and thigh bone. The front ligament (the anterior) is far more likely to suffer damage than the rear one (the posterior).

Symptoms: Searing pain from inside the knee – you will not be able to support yourself on that leg – swelling and discolouration.

Causes: These ligaments hold the knee joint together from within, so twisting it or moving it backwards, suddenly and with the force of your weight on it, will damage it.

Self-help: Get off that leg immediately and apply R.I.C.E. If the tissue is stretched rather than torn, icing the area and resting it, maybe for a few weeks, could be sufficient. If, however, it doesn't start to settle down after a couple of weeks, seek medical advice as it may be ruptured and could require surgery.

Prevention: Well-developed hamstrings will help guard against cruciate ligament damage, as those muscles stabilize the knee joint in much the same way as the connective tissue does.

Lateral meniscus tear

Injury to the crescent-shaped piece of cartilage that sits in the knee joint between the shin bone and the thigh bone. (There are

Recovery time

It takes most runners at least 24 hours to recover from a good run (48 if they're over forty). During that time all the little niggles, knocks and muscle tears that you might not consciously feel are repairing themselves. To cut short this time between sessions is to inflict new damage to things that haven't mended properly yet.

two cartilage menisci within the knee, but the other, the medial meniscus, is far less prone to injury.)

Symptoms: Intense pain from within the knee – often confused with cruciate ligament injury. Frequently, meniscus damage will produce an audible clicking sound from the knee and the inability to fully straighten the leg, because a detached piece of cartilage is obstructing the joint. Swelling starts several hours later.

Causes: Because these cartilages act as shock absorbers, distributing the impact of the stride into the thighs, they are susceptible to damage from high impact or twisting out of line. The meniscus cartilage may well get damaged at the same time as a knee joint suffers cruciate or collateral ligament injury.

Self-help: R.I.C.E. Or, if it is serious and is not responding to rest and ice, it may require surgery to remove detached cartilage and rebuild the interior of the joint.

Prevention: Little can be done by way of prevention, but strong quads and hamstrings will make sure the knee is held stable.

Runner's knee

Also called chrondromalacia, it is caused by friction between the inside of the kneecap and the knee itself as the joint flexes.

Symptoms: Sharp pain from inside or alongside the knee as it flexes; it will sometimes swell up.

Causes: Weak quads that are unable to hold the kneecap in place allowing it to shift and rub; tight hamstrings that work against the quads; over-pronation throwing the lower leg out of whack; overtraining, meaning the quads are too tired to hold the kneecap in its correct place.

Self-help: R.I.C.E. You can run through it, but you should ice the knee for fifteen minutes as soon as you have cooled down.

Prevention: Thorough stretching of the quads, hamstrings and glutes; keep the quads well developed with strength training exercises (see p.126–129); run in the correct shoes.

Tip: Runner's knee sufferers should avoid kneeling down or squatting with knees fully bent. They should also sit with their legs out straight whenever possible.

Fact: If you are a runner's knee sufferer, strapping the joint before running will not make much difference.

Hips, groin and thighs

Central to keeping your whole body aligned, the hips absorb and correct a great deal of what might be wrong elsewhere. This often manifests itself in injuries within that area such as sciatica, lower back pain or piriformis syndrome. Also, with five separate bones and four main ligaments performing seven different movements, it is vulnerable to its own internal damage through tension and impact. It is vital to loosen the hips and the iliotibial band with dynamic stretching before you set off.

Muscle balance is vital for the larger muscles of the upper legs. Although it is the rear muscles that power your stride – calves, hamstrings, glutes – their opposite numbers in the front of the legs have to be equally maintained to avoid strain.

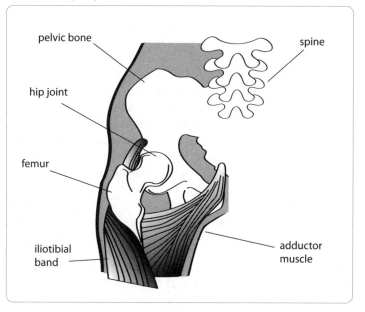

Adductor strain (also known as groin strain)

Tearing or straining of the muscle that runs down the inside of the thigh, where the thigh bone joins the pubic bone.

Symptoms: Swelling or tenderness on the inside of the thigh and pain when the leg is moved inwards or outwards – this is the muscle group responsible for the hip joint's lateral stability.

Causes: Sudden sideways movement pulling the upper leg outwards, as can occur when running over uneven ground or cross-country. Damage can also occur over time if your gait throws the hip joint out of line – badly worn shoes might do this.

Self-help: R.I.C.E. and a lay off until it recovers – this injury can get considerably worse if you attempt to run through it.

Prevention: Stretch the muscle out properly, using the groin stretch exercise (see p.88).

Hamstring (pulled)

The tearing of the muscle fibres at the rear of the thigh – much more common in sprinting than in distance running.

Symptoms: These will depend on the severity of the tears. Pain at the rear of the thigh followed by bruising and swelling will be a given, but there is the possibility of muscle spasm or the inability to contract and expand the muscle to bend the knee.

Causes: The muscle has either been overloaded or moved too fast too suddenly, or has suffered an "eccentric contraction", in which it has attempted to contract and an outside influence – the ground, somebody else – has either stopped that contraction or actively lengthened the muscle.

Self-help: Stop running immediately, apply R.I.C.E. and stay off the leg as much as possible. Attempt to gently stretch the muscle out, and if straightening is either painful or impossible, get medical advice. When starting to run again while recovering, it is advisable to wear an elastic support bandage to compress the thigh muscles and so not place them under undue stress.

Prevention: These injuries are so unpredictable that they are difficult to prevent, but well-stretched, properly warmed up muscle will always be less susceptible to such damage.

Hip bursitis

Inflammation of one of the hip joint's two bursae (fluid-filled sacs), which then rubs across the tendon as you stride, causing irritation.
Symptoms: Stabbing pain at either the outside of the hip or the top of the buttock that will be consistent with activity.
Causes: An over-use injury, usually caused by running on shoes with no cushioning ability. It can be aggravated (sometimes even caused) by sitting in the same position for long stretches.
Self-help: Ice to reduce the bursae's swelling, then no more running until pain no longer occurs. Because the bursae are practically inside the joint they will receive impact every time you hit the ground, therefore this is not an injury that can be run off.
Prevention: Make sure your shoes are fully functional and switch to softer surfaces.

Iliotibial band syndrome (ITBS)

The inflammation of the thick band of tissue running outside the knee that connects the hip bone to the shin bone.
Symptoms: Pain at the outside of the knee, or down the outside of the thigh.
Causes: Instead of running smoothly over the outside of the knee joint, the swollen tissue rubs, causing the pain. The most common causes are overtraining or running with insufficient rest periods, meaning the iliotibial band cannot properly recover from the pounding it takes. Also, over-pronators are susceptible to it as the inward rolling of the gait stresses the tissue around the kneecap.
Self-help: As this is usually an over-use injury, ice and rest, then easing back on the running. When you're ready to start back up again, gently stretch out the band to ease the discomfort.
Prevention: A static stretching routine that concentrates on the

Tip: Go in for regular routine maintenance. In the same way as you have your car serviced, visit a sports-knowledgeable osteopath or chiropractor two or three times a year, whether you think you need it or not, just to make sure everything is working as well as it should be.

iliotibial band will ease it out so it can move freely around that joint. The correct shoes and staying off uneven surfaces will help enormously. Strengthening the iliotibial band to keep it more stable while running reduces the effect of stride impact – if recovering from ITBS and not running your usual distances, keep the muscle built up with relevant non-impact crosstraining.

Lower back pain

Symptoms: Pain in the small of your back or anywhere along the six inches or so above your buttocks.

Causes: Anything that distributes weight unevenly above the pelvis, such as over-pronation or leg length discrepancy, can lead to lower back pain. Tight hamstrings can put stress on that area, too. Weak abdominal muscles can also mean the lower back is absorbing too much of the impact shock that is transmitted up through the legs, while worn-out shoes can contribute to all these causes.

Self-help: R.I.C.E. and massage are good for lower back pain, as is gentle stretching. Avoid running on steep hills as this will alter your posture and possibly aggravate your lower back.

Prevention: Strengthening abdominal muscles will provide support for the lower back, which together with regular stretching and pre-run loosening of the area will help absorb the impact from each stride. The correct shoes will also take pressure off.

Quadriceps injuries

Commonly known as "thigh strain", tearing in one of the four muscles that make up the quads – most commonly the rectus femoris, the one most visible under the skin in the front.

Symptoms: Mild quad strain will mean a tightness down the front of the thigh; medium strain will mean a sharp twinge of pain; a bad strain causes severe pain. In the first case, the symptoms might not show until after your run and then might be confused with DOMS (see p.179). In more serious cases you will not be able to carry on running with any comfort, and the affected area will swell up.

Causes: More common in sprinting and sports that involve explosive bursts of leg speed than in distance running, the tears happen when the muscle is stretched beyond its limit.

Self-help: All but the most severe cases can be treated with R.I.C.E. and deep tissue massage (see p.81). You should also take a break from running for between three and six weeks. Complete ruptures of the muscle, however, will require surgery.

Prevention: Stretch quads properly during warm-up and if you are susceptible to or recovering from quad strain, wear knee-length compression shorts.

Sciatica

The compression or irritation of the sciatic nerve.

Symptoms: Numbness or electric shock-type pains in the buttocks or lower back, which can extend down the back of the entire leg.

Causes: The sciatic nerve is a main channel of the nervous system running down the lower spine through the legs to the feet, and a number of extraneous factors can cause it problems: uneven running posture throwing the pelvis out of line; tense glutes, hamstrings, calves or iliotibial bands; a damaged vertebra; friction between thigh and groin muscles... The pain won't necessarily be in the same place as the problem.

Self-help: This is one you don't treat with R.I.C.E., but – and this is the only time I'll recommend them – with pain killers, anti-inflammatories and keeping mobile as sitting for long periods can aggravate sciatica. Spine stretching exercises can help relieve pain in the nerve. Once that has been done, you need to find out the cause of your sciatica and treat that.

Prevention: Compression shorts separate the thigh and groin muscles, while spine and muscle stretching will remove tension.

Other stuff

As a runner, don't neglect your spine, your neck and your shoulders. These are also liable to tension-related and over-use injuries that can be serious in the long term, painful in the short term, or both. There are also a bunch of general maladies you shouldn't ignore.

Chafing

Rubbing of body parts or clothing that causes friction – not just the preserve of fat runners. (See also Runner's nipple and Sciatica).

Symptoms: Irritated patches of skin that might be rubbed raw.

Causes: Body parts – inside of thighs, armpits or groin in particular – rubbing together as you stride, or clothing causing friction against skin. This can be made considerably worse if those garments are cotton and drenched in sweat, or the sweat is drying on the skin leaving an abrasive coating of salt. This will sting horribly if it gets into contact with a raw patch of skin.

Self-help: Apply Vaseline to areas that are chafing, and an antiseptic cream to any patches that have been rubbed raw.

Prevention: Apply Vaseline before you set off, wear properly fitting wicking clothing and stay hydrated so your sweat keeps flowing – that way it won't dry up and leave a layer of salt on your skin.

So sodium

Time was when loss of salt through sweat was a big problem for a distance runner, as it could lead to cramp. Nowadays, however, the average Western diet has around three times the daily recommended level of salt, and for a runner to take on board extra could cause serious problems. High levels of sodium in the system raise blood pressure, which could become dangerous when a runner's heart rate rises. Also, it will block the absorption of calcium while increasing the amount secreted, which will weaken bones and inhibit the repair of calcified cartilage. Unless you know you have a low-salt diet, avoid the sports drinks with a higher sodium content.

Cramp

A contracted muscle that goes into spasm and will not relax.

Symptoms: A stabbing pain in the affected muscle that can vary in severity and duration; the inability to straighten that muscle.

Causes: As a distance runner you're mostly likely to get cramp because of fatigue, dehydration combined with salt deficiency, or lack of overall fitness.

Self-help: Gentle stretching and progressive deep massage along the length of the muscle fibres to help them relax; rehydration.

Prevention: Warm up and stretch thoroughly, make sure you have taken on sufficient fluids and don't go too far over your limits.

Delayed Onset Muscle Soreness (DOMS)

Pretty much what it says on the tin – muscle soreness that is felt between 24 and 72 hours after exercising.

Symptoms: Aches and pains in muscles that were exercised.

Causes: The microscopic tearing of the exercised muscles causes the pain but it's believed this damage doesn't cause a breakdown in the muscle protein until exercise has stopped. Hence it will be at its worst the next day. New exercises or running greater distances are obvious reasons, as muscles will be worked in a way they're not used to. There is a popular theory that eccentric contractions during exercise (lengthening while under tension – lowering a curl, walking downstairs, running downhill) cause more DOMS than concentric contractions (muscles shortening while under tension).

Self-help: R.I.C.E. Avoid using affected muscle until pain passes, but during that time perform gentle stretching and massage on it.

Prevention: Warm up thoroughly and cool down properly, stretching muscles out while still warm. Build up intensity slowly.

Heat exhaustion

The body overheating.

Symptoms: Thirst, dizziness, headache, disorientation, nausea. Heat exhaustion can lead to potentially fatal heatstroke (see p.35).

> **Tip:** If after a long run you get bad DOMS in your hamstrings and walking downstairs is very painful, go down backwards – it won't hurt nearly so much.

Causes: When lack of fluid intake combines with increased sweating it leads to severe dehydration and the body's internal temperature soars.

Self-help: Stop running and get out of the sun, preferably somewhere cool. Take on water or sports drinks (see p.36), but drink them slowly; don't gulp or you will probably throw it back up.

Prevention: In warmer weather make sure you are properly hydrated before setting off, then take on fluids regularly throughout your run and continue to do so for some time afterwards.

Neck pain 1 (radiating out from the neck)
Symptoms: Ache or shooting pains spreading through the shoulders and maybe resulting in a tingling in the fingers.

Causes: Trapped nerve or spinal disc damage

Self-help: A nerve will usually be trapped by tense muscles and can be freed by relaxing the neck with gentle stretching and massage. If you suspect disc damage, this is much more serious and you should seek medical advice.

Prevention: Regular and gentle neck stretching will keep it loose, then be careful not to let your neck tense up as you run.

Neck pain 2 (remaining in neck)
Symptoms: Sharp pain extending no further than the neck; stiffening of the neck; and pain when turning the head.

Causes: Neck muscles are too tense.

Self-help: Relax the neck with gentle stretching and massage.

Prevention: Keep neck relaxed when running.

Runner's nipple
Chafing of the nipples while running.

Symptoms: Sore, sometimes bloody nipples – may not even be noticed until a particularly painful shower after your run.

Causes: Rubbing of the shirt across the chest, usually because it is a) tight fitting; b) cotton soaked in abrasive, salty sweat; c) one with a screen-printed design across the chest; d) all of the above.

Tip: Attempting to mask your nipples with sticking plaster may work for children's TV presenters, but it is worse than useless for runners – it either won't stick to your chest hair or will irritatingly start to come adrift as you warm up and start sweating.

Self-help: Smear a dollop of Vaseline across over each nipple and make sure you replenish it as your run progresses as it will melt and run offf as you start to sweat – most well-organized races have people along the route holding trays laden with trays of dabs of petroleum jelly.

Prevention: Wear a looser, lighter, moisture-control shirt, and apply petroleum jelly before you set off.

Side stitches

The straining of the ligaments that connect the diaphragm to the liver and other internal organs.

Symptoms: Sharp, stabbing pain just beneath the rib cage, usually on the right-hand side.

Causes: Running's jolting motion and the interaction between the internal organs and the diaphragm. If you're breathing out (pulling the diaphragm up) as the right foot lands and the liver (the largest and heaviest organ), which is on that side, moves down with the stride's motion, the connecting ligament will become over extended. Most runners naturally exhale when landing their left feet – the minority who don't are far more prone to side stitches.

Self-help: Stop running or slow to a walk, push fingers up on lower right hand side of stomach to lift liver, breathe deeply and evenly. Stretch out the ligaments by raising your right arm straight up and slowly leaning to the left into a stretch, hold for twenty seconds, repeat with left arm.

Prevention: Breathe deeply to make sure the diaphragm gets fully lowered and completely extends the ligament – side stitches are particularly common in beginners who tend to breathe less deeply and have yet to develop a smooth technique. Alter your breathing pattern to exhale when striking with your left foot. Don't eat within two hours of running, as a full and therefore heavier stomach will put added stress on those ligaments, but make sure you have plenty of water as dehydrated tissue is much more likely to cramp up.

Running
for real

Second-stage motivation

9

You've hit your initial targets, raised your fitness levels and suddenly it's all got a bit "So what?".

Congratulations, you've just reached running's second stage.

You've achieved a great deal in a relatively short space of time, but now, having reached those goals, you've reduced your reasons to run and motivational difficulties will start to rear up.

However, it's also time to make the jump to the next level and really power up your running, as there's now even more to aim for and get excited about. This chapter will help you motivate yourself.

Take a good look at your running

If your interest levels start to drop off at this stage, the basis of your re-motivation has to lie in what it is you really want out of running, beyond what you have already achieved. This sort of self-awareness is the singularly most neglected area of all runners' approach to their sport. Runners run, they rarely think about why they are running and what running means to their minds and bodies, which does not form a sound basis for improvement. Taking this look at yourself as a runner is the first step towards understanding what you are actually doing. But you will need to take a general view, rather than thinking about it in terms of specific goals. The first step is to establish your running personality – whether you are an "intrinsic" or an "extrinsic" runner.

What sort of runner are you?

> **//** I've run many miles by myself, and although the solitude can be great and it's good to challenge yourself and push yourself on, running with other people is much better. It's more sociable, it's safer, you find out new routes, it's seldom boring and you have someone else to motivate and support you and to run against. Sometimes it's also good to support others and worry less about your own problems. The miles pass more quickly in company. **//**
> **Karen Hancock**

• For the **intrinsic runner**, running is personal and spiritual. It is about inner peace and solitude, communing with the elements and

gaining an inherent satisfaction from the sights, sounds and sensations of running. If an intrinsic runner competes, they do so against themselves, because satisfaction and a sense of achievement come from within rather than from timings on a board. Most intrinsic runners wouldn't be too bothered if they never went running in a group or a race field again.

• The **extrinsic runner** is a far more sociable character when it comes to hitting the bricks, and will gain running satisfaction from being in a group and comparing themselves to others. Although they won't be unaware of the more Zen aspects of running, their real kick comes in how their running relates to other people's.

Once you've established which kind of runner you are, it will be far easier to plan your running life around the aspects that inspire you and to ignore what is likely to put you off.

Intrinsic runners should look to make their running as sensory, as spiritually uplifting, as downright interesting and as personally challenging as possible, entering races for the experience of the whole event rather than worrying about setting a new personal best (see pp.215–217). Then types of running (see pp.21–26), or the *Rough Guide* travel book catalogue should provide plenty of food for thought.

Extrinsic runners can give themselves a considerable motivational boost by entering races (see pp.201–217) or by joining a running club or group (see below). Don't assume you'll have to miss out on the travelling either, as there are many exciting and highly competitive races around the world – see our listings on pp.247–250.

Join the club

Even if you are essentially an intrinsic runner, there are an enormous number of advantages to be gained from joining a running club at this stage of your development. Running as a group can provide the motivational push to get you on to the next level and you will pick up all sorts of training tips as fellow members share information. It can also help you establish a running routine. Remember, you can always go back to solo running any time you like.

Running groups are by nature informal – like-minded souls who meet at a prescribed time and place and go for a run. Before joining

> *There's a great deal to be gained from joining a running club, but it has to be the right club. Too many people join a club that, for whatever reason, isn't right for them and it puts them off running. Go along to a few sessions before committing to join to see if it's the right sort of atmosphere for you.*
> **Karen Hancock**

Tip: If your offices have shower facilities, your work colleagues can make up an ideal lunchtime running group. Send a company-wide email or put up a notice by the coffee machine.

> *Beginners worry, when joining a club, that they won't be good enough or that everybody's going to laugh at them. That's why it's important to find one that genuinely does cater for beginners. Not all do, but the bigger the club, the more likely you are to find company for your running.*
> **Karen Hancock**

Tip: Your local running shop should have details of running clubs and groups in the area. They may even have a noticeboard to allow runners to get in touch with each other.

// Running clubs are great for motivation, training and the social side of running, but be careful if you enter a race with other people – make sure you run at your pace and don't be sucked in to running at somebody else's. It never ever works.
Efua Baker //

To find a running club or group near you, check out:

www.running.timeoutdoors.com/clubs

www.running4women.com

one, make sure it is of the desired standard as regards distance and timings, as most groups have set distances and pace and there's no point in hooking up with runners who are much too fast for you or won't be going far enough for you to warm up properly. The larger, more structured running clubs will offer training programmes, different levels of running, race preparation often leading to group entry, newsletters, forums, exclusive website access, events, coaching advice and maybe even club merchandise. This will probably come with a membership fee, though, so it is vital you find out exactly what you will be getting for your money – outlay will often be recouped through club discounts on race entries.

Do it yourself

If you can't find a running club or group that meets your needs, start your own. Begin informally by setting a location and time that suits you, but isn't entirely unsociable, and advertise it with a notice in your local running shop or on a runners' forum-type website. Even if only one other person turns up, you'll be better off than you were.

Write it down

It might sound a bit old hat but, at a time like this when all you really need to do is remind yourself of how good it is to run, physically writing down the reasons why you run really does work. Divide a couple of blank sheets of paper down the middle and on the left-hand side of one sheet list every way in which you have benefited since you started running (weight loss, no hangovers, more alert, etc). Then, on the opposite side, list everything bad that's happened to you as a result of running (twisted ankle, er…). On the second sheet, list reasons why you should continue with running against reasons why you should pack it in (ie stay fitter, reduce the chance of heart disease, meet interesting people versus, well, nothing at all). I can guarantee that in every case the left-hand list will be much longer than its right-hand counterpart.

Mood music

Which type of music is best to run to is a debate without even a sign of an end, and such a degree of subjectivity means everybody has their favourite running playlist (1940s big band jazz and 1970s jazz/funk works for me every time). If you are experiencing motivational problems in your running life, play that soundtrack at home, as often as possible and as loudly as is feasible. It will immediately trigger memories of running and provide a powerful reminder of how much enjoyment you have got out of it.

Keep it interesting

One of the reasons running might feel like a bit of a chore by now is because you've let it become one. At this stage, when the initial motivation of becoming a runner has played itself out, running essentially the same route in pretty much the same times can get awfully tedious, awfully quickly. It's worth putting some effort into keeping your running interesting, and that can sometimes mean more than just the actual running.

Tip: If running home from work, don't worry about getting odd looks from other commuters – you'll be home before them!

1. Looking good, feeling good

Invest in some flashy, high-tech running kit. It's amazing what an effect this will have on your runs as you quite unwittingly start to show off. Besides, you deserve a reward for getting this far.

2. Sponsor yourself

Put a set amount of money in a jar for every mile you run, then use it to treat yourself to something not immediately associated with running. Treats could include a case of wine, a box of cigars, a plasma screen TV or a long weekend away.

3. Run to somewhere or from somewhere

If you've got showers at work and it's a realistic distance, run in in the morning – you'll arrive invigorated and with more money in

your pocket. Or, run home at the end of the day. You'll find you enjoy your evening more and will sleep better.

4. Use your running time constructively

When else will you get an hour or two just to yourself, in the fresh air, with few distractions? Running time is the best thinking time you'll ever get.

5. Set yourself a schedule

Knowing you've got to do a prescribed number of miles each week, striving to get better and then being able to follow a record of improvements in time and distance can be a powerful motivator for some people.

6. Tear up your schedule

However, the less ambitious/competitive among you might find the notion of keeping records too much pressure, so ditch the training log and get back to running for fun.

> When I first came to London in 2001 I didn't know anybody. Then I joined the Serpies (The Serpentine Running Club), which is a very big club, and now I'm always bumping into people I know through running.
> **Karen Hancock**

7. Play games

Race buses, time yourself between set points, see how far you dare to run backwards, count different types of cars, chase dogs, play I-spy… there are all sorts of essentially puerile but quite entertaining games you can play as you run.

8. Get lost

Take a different turning or go off your regular route just to see where it leads. You can always turn round and come back if you're not keen on where you seem to be heading.

9. Have a laugh

Smile while you're running and greet other runners and pedestrians. You can have a great deal of fun watching people recoil in embarrassment from such random acts of pleasantry.

10. Don't even think about it

Much as we love it, the mechanical act of running is dead boring, and if you start thinking about it while you're doing it you tend to dwell on aches and pains or how far you've got left to do. Let your feet do their stuff while you get on with points 4 or 7 or 9…

Tip: When evaluating your running, don't forget to keep it in the context of your life. Your circumstances away from running will have a great deal to do with how you approach the road.

Goooaaal(s)!

If staying motivated is the mental aspect of second-stage running, then setting goals is the physical manifestation of it.

Setting goals is the difference between simply telling yourself you are going to run as fast as you can for the next three-quarters of an hour or so and vowing to run a sub-45 minute 10k in three months' time. Having a realistic but challenging target to aim for focuses the mind and gives you a tangible road map along which to chart your progression. This chapter examines how to set goals and how best to then achieve them.

Types of goal

To attempt to move forward as a runner without some sort of solid objective would be extremely difficult, if not impossible, and the most important rule of goal setting – in any field, not just running – is that you are able to define that goal. Even if your objective is no more complicated than to keep running for as many years as possible, to stay fit and keep your weight down, once you are focused on it you can work out how best to run to make sure you achieve that goal.

There are three different types of goal a runner should concern themselves with. The first, process goals, you will already have achieved by getting this far. Process goals are all about becoming proficient at a particular skill or action – the term refers to coming to grips with the actual process rather than what you do with it once you have mastered it. At this point you should be setting yourself either performance or outcome goals.

Performance goals are recommended for second-stage runners, as they are about what you can achieve with your new skills: for example, you want to run a sub-25-minute 5k in three months' time, or you're going to build up to running thirty miles a week by Christmas. These goals depend pretty much solely on what you put in – training, diet, motivation, dedication – therefore they are about your performance in isolation rather than in relation to others. They can boost your self-awareness as they vividly illustrate running's straightforward effort/reward equation. Also, achieving a series of goals while still relatively new to any sport is great for your self-confidence.

Developing goals is the best way to keep you running, but only if they are the right goals. The wrong ones will just as quickly discourage you

Outcome goals are best left to the big dogs for the time being, as they will be objectives such as "I'm going to finish in the first three in next year's New York Marathon" or "I'm going to be the best in my age group in the Great North Run". In terms of achievability they are for those already at the top of their game, elite runners whose motivation for entering races isn't just to finish but who have a realistic chance of stepping onto the podium. Even at a lower level, outcome goals are a recipe for frustration as they take the achievement out of your hands by being dependent on your beating other people – you could run a fantastic race, but five other people might just run even better.

Tip: As a motivational tool, set one of your frequently used PIN numbers as your target time, and you will be regularly reminded of what you hope to achieve.

Just to keep you focused...

Here are the IAAF world records, correct at the time of writing:

Distance	Men	Women
Mile	3 min 43.13 s	4 min 12.56 s
5k	12 min 37.35 s	14 min 24.53 s
10k	27 min 02 s	30 min 21 s
Half marathon	58 min 35 s	1 hr 6 min 44 s
Marathon	2 hr 4 min 55 s	2 hr 15 min 25 s

Tip: Even though you should talk to other runners as you decide on your goals, this is strictly for advice. Always be sure you are deciding on your own goals and not somebody else's.

Think it through

Don't just pull your goal out of the air. Spend time working out exactly what it should be. You should base it less on what level you'd like to reach and more on what level of fitness and ability you are currently at. Work out exactly what it is you want out of running at this stage – weight loss, fitness, running as a sport, improvement in another sport – then start by looking at the best way to achieve that. Be prepared to do some research too: study the training schedules and tips in this book, talk to other runners, look up records for

www.runnersworld.co.uk has a very lively and helpful online forum, where runners around the globe swap tips, discuss difficulties they might be having and share experiences.

gooooaaal(s)!

Fact: Less will always be more if it means you stay free from injury.

the range of distances you are interested in (for reference, *not* as a target!), check out the many running training websites, and generally use other runners' experience to find out what you should be aiming for. Then, factor in such extraneous influences as the time of year, how much time is available and what sort of obligations you have in your real life as opposed to your running life. Only when you have put all of this together will you be able to get an accurate idea of what your goals ought to be. Even then you'll need to build in some sort of contingency plan in case you get injured or hit a bad run of weather because, although you will be taking your goal seriously, the best plans have a bit of flexibility in them.

Precisely measurable

What you have decided upon cannot be woolly or vague. Your goals have to be precisely quantifiable and perfectly measurable – "I'm going to run six or seven miles in an hour or so!" just won't do. By treating it as an exact science you'll be able to measure even the smallest improvements, which is vital because some days your progress will be minute yet still deserving to be logged.

Tip: To plot your steps towards your goal, adapt a training log (pp.124–125) to focus on looking forward to an achievement rather than just recording what has already been done.

This brings us to another important point – write it all down. Recording your relentless slog towards your goal is as crucial as achieving the goal itself, if for no other reason than to keep you going.

Fact: Goal-setting helps enormously with your self-awareness as a runner as it forces you to constantly think about what you are doing.

Beyond the comfort zone

The "no pain, no gain" method should have no place in your running world, but that doesn't mean things should be too comfortable. Realistic goal setting is about aiming for something outside the realms of your usual performances but still entirely attainable. You need to be stretching yourself – otherwise what's the point? – but always beware of going for over-ambitious targets, as that can so often lead to over-training and all that goes with it.

The sort of improvement you should be looking for would be to knock thirty seconds or a full minute off your time for one kilometre, which should be challenging enough to hold your interest, but still be very possible. But while it might not seem like much when written like that, multiply it by ten and you'll find it could make a great deal of difference to your race day timings.

Bit by bit by bit

Once you have decided on your goal, break it down into manageable segments, or a series of smaller aims – goalettes? For instance, if you set a goal of running 10k no slower than five minutes per kilometre within three months, and at the moment you're running it at more than six, you can structure a series of milestones to aim for over shorter periods of time. Devise a speed programme that will get you down to below six minutes after one month, below five-and-a-half at the end of the second month, then faster than five at three months. You can even break it down into smaller increments and aim to pass defined markers on a weekly basis.

Working towards your goals as a series of performance plateaus makes the whole process much more manageable, as the hill you've set yourself to climb won't seem nearly so steep. Then, because you

Fact: Entering and preparing for a race is an ideal goal to set yourself, and it doesn't matter if you don't think of yourself as a competitive runner. For the vast majority of runners the notion of where they might finish never enters into the equation, and they are simply there for the event.

Play it S.M.A.R.T.
When setting goals for yourself they should be:
Specific
Measurable
Achievable
Realistic
Time sensitive

Tip: Don't expect to rush your goals. If you achieve them well within the set time they probably weren't difficult enough.

> When you set your goals, break them down into a series of smaller achievements. That way, as you run, you will feel yourself constantly going onwards and upwards.
> **Karen Hancock**

Fact: The fitter you are, the less likely you are to improve. Everybody has a level past which they cannot be pushed.

can start achieving almost immediately, there will be a strong sense of accomplishment, meaning motivation shouldn't be too much of a problem. Also, because this step-by-step plan is being constantly assessed, if your ultimate goal proves to be too difficult or too easy you will soon find out and be able to reset your sights.

Stay positive

When thinking about how you're progressing with your current goal, focus on what you have achieved rather than what you haven't. This may be difficult when you're keeping a log and entries that don't reach your target seem to be taunting you from the page, but concentrate on the improvements you have make.

If you are consistently falling short then you've probably set the bar too high and it should be adjusted accordingly. It's because of their massive potential for frustration that outcome goals (see p.194) are seldom recommended for the majority of runners.

Enjoy the process as well as the end result

Although challenging yourself by setting goals is what will raise your performance, don't let it rule your running life. The important thing about your running is to enjoy yourself, and if goal setting is putting too much pressure on you then scale it back or take a rest from it for a while.

Also, the journey to improvement should be as pleasurable as the achievement itself, with each increment a cause for its own celebration. Then, once you've reached your goal, it's perfectly excusable to rest on your laurels for a few months before starting to consider the next goal. Look at the very big picture and think of your entire running life as a goal in itself, and the objective you have just achieved as one of the staging posts along the way.

Wanna race?

Of course you do.

Whatever your reasons for taking up running, the fact that you're still doing it after a prolonged period of time means you're pretty serious. And serious runners go in for races. This chapter looks at how to enter, how to prepare for and how to run one, not forgetting what you ought to be doing on the following couple of days.

One of the most encouraging things about the current running climate is that there are so many races taking place and nearly half of all the UK's runners have entered at least one event.

Entering your first race is fantastic motivation for you to take your running up a gear, as you will feel much more psychologically involved. From the moment you've submitted your application you'll have a set goal and will have given yourself a rigidly defined amount of time to prepare for it. Now you can draw up a training schedule (see pp.205–206) that has a real sense of purpose. It's remarkable what a zip this will put in your running as, suddenly, it becomes anything other than aimless.

Run for fun

The biggest growth area in running all around the world is the fun run scene. Although these events are technically termed "races", the majority of entrants are not there to try to win anything, but to experience the camaraderie of doing something fit and healthy as part of a field of several thousand. The races are more like huge, mobile social gatherings with many runners aiming simply to finish the distance and only then giving any thought to timing or placing. It's this party atmosphere around so many of the high-profile races that's a huge factor in attracting people to running, which in turn is creating more and bigger events, perpetuating this informal party atmosphere. All of which is as good for running in general as it is for you.

Know when you are ready to enter your first race

You will be ready to enter a race as soon as you start thinking about entering a race. It's that simple. If you're serious enough about your running to be considering something other than just pounding the pavements, then you should definitely be entering races.

There are so many organized runs of a mile and upwards taking place all over the country these days that it will be easy to find

It's the taking part that counts. Honestly it is!

Going in for fun run events is where running agreeably blurs the edges between a sport and a pastime, and you can be as competitive as you want to be. So at this stage, don't worry if you're slow or have to walk a couple of kilometres – you'll do better next time. Because there's bound to be a next time…

Run for money

The rise in charity running is the biggest driving force behind the current fun run expansion, and it's easy to take part. Events like Race For Life (**www.raceforlife.org**) are organized in aid of specific charities, while other charities "buy up" entries to big races like the New York marathon and offer places, often with fares paid, to runners who'll pledge to raise a prescribed sum (*Runner's World* magazine always features advertisements for these). Alternatively, you can simply organize things yourself at **www.justgiving.com**, a one-stop shop for raising sponsorship. They have a list of over 2,000 good causes, and will set you up a page so your friends can sponsor you online.

an event that a) is convenient, and b) you feel confident you can complete. And, well, that's about it. It's unlikely you'll win any event you enter but you've probably already worked that one out. For the vast majority of us runners, we'll never win anything other than a healthier, more enjoyable lifestyle and the undying respect of our peers – but that won't stop us entering races.

Entering your first race

The most important consideration is whether you'll be able to get to the course easily on race day - probably a Sunday morning. The last thing you need is to have to leave your house unnecessarily early and endure a stressful journey or problems parking.

Next, decide on what distance you want to go for. Ideally it should be a distance you have already covered as that will greatly reduce any worries about finishing the course. Or, if you are an absolute beginner, choose a distance you're pretty certain you could handle – just about anybody in reasonable health could finish a 5k, or, given a few months to prepare, a 10k. If you haven't previously done anything near the distance you've selected, you will do best to stick to a prescribed training schedule.

> **//** Not everybody can run a marathon, and it shouldn't be seen as something you have to do to prove yourself as a runner. So many runners are naturally much better suited to shorter distances and should stick to them. **//**
> **Karen Hancock**

> **❝** The main thing to remember when entering your first race is to remain confident that you're not going to come last. Then once you've done one, the subsequent races will be much easier. **❞**
> **Hugh Jones**

Then don't dither! Once you have made up your mind to enter a specific event, get the forms in as quickly as possible – although there are literally hundreds of races each year in the UK, there are hundreds of thousands of runners and most events don't take long to fill up. It will be necessary to plan ahead, as the biggest events are really popular. On the plus side, this means you will have longer to train and prepare for the event, and assuming the first race you enter is a 5k or 10k – by far the most popular distances for first-time racers – three months will be plenty of time to go through a training programme.

The following two training schedules are for 5k and 10k. Both assume a reasonable level of relative running fitness – ie you could handle the distance involved at a steady pace. The 5k schedule picks up from where you ought to be if you have followed our first and second-stage training programmes (see pp.18–20) and then carried on running regularly for at least a couple of months. The 10k schedule assumes that you can already run a decent 5k, ie in something under 30 minutes. Both will take you right up to race day, and the key to them – indeed to any good race training schedule – is making sure you build up slowly and allow plenty of time for rest and recovery.

Race training psychology

> **❝** As far as motivation for that first race goes, it will have been an awful lot harder to motivate yourself to actually start running – by this point you'll be in a steady routine. **❞**
> **Hugh Jones**

Once you start training for a race you'll discover how much running has to offer mentally as well as physically. You'll be amazed at how much mental effort you find yourself putting in because pushing yourself that little bit further on a regular basis requires great focus. Even the determination needed to get out there whatever the weather and not leave any shameful blank spaces in your training log involves a degree of fortitude. As you progress, you'll continue to exercise this mental strength as you'll be entering

Six-week 5k training schedule

	Monday	Tuesday	Wednesday	Thursday	Friday	Saturday	Sunday
Week 1	Rest	15 min regular; 10 min Fartlek; 15 min regular	Rest	10 min regular; 4 x 500m flat out with 2 min jogging in between; 10 min regular	Rest	30 min regular	10 min regular; 10 min race pace; 10 min regular
Week 2	Rest	35 min regular	Rest	10 min regular; 10 min 1 min/k faster than race pace; 10 min regular	Rest	35 min regular	10 min regular; 5 x 500m flat out with 2 min jog in between; 10 min regular
Week 3	Rest	40 min regular	Rest	15 min regular; 10 min 1 min/k faster than race pace; 10 min regular	Rest	40 min regular	5 min regular; 20 min race pace; 5 min regular
Week 4	Rest	40 min regular	Rest	10 min regular; 20 min Fartlek; 10 min regular	Rest	45 min regular	10 min regular; 6 x 500m flat out with 2 min jog in between; 10 min regular
Week 5	Rest	40 min regular	Rest	10 min regular; 15 min 1 min/k faster than race pace; 10 min regular	Rest	35 min regular	30 min race pace
Week 6	Rest	30 min regular	Rest	15 min regular; 15 min Fartlek; 15 min regular	Rest	20 min very easy, including stride-outs	Race Day

Six-week 10k training schedule

	Monday	Tuesday	Wednesday	Thursday	Friday	Saturday	Sunday
Week 1	Rest	15 min regular; 20 min Fartlek; 15 min regular	Rest	10 min regular; 5k at 5k race pace; 5 min regular	Rest	60 min regular	10 min regular; 4 x 800m flat out with 2 min jog in between; 10 min regular
Week 2	Rest	60 min regular	Rest	15 min regular; 20 min 1 min/k faster than 10k race pace; 15 min regular	Rest	60 min regular	15 min regular; 20 min 1 min/k faster than 10k race pace; 15 min regular
Week 3	Rest	65 min regular	Rest	20 min regular; 25 min Fartlek; 20 min regular	Rest	65 min regular	15 min regular; 20 min 1 min/k faster than 10k race pace; 20 min regular
Week 4	Rest	65 min regular	Rest	15 min regular; 5 X 800m flat out with 2 min jog in between; 10 min regular	Rest	65 min regular	15 min regular; 20 min 1 min/k faster than 10k race pace; 20 min regular
Week 5	Rest	70 min regular	Rest	15 min regular; 30 min 1 min/k faster than 10k race pace; 20 min regular	Rest	70 min regular	15 min regular; 5k at 5k race pace; 15 min regular
Week 6	Rest	60 min regular	Rest	20 min regular; 20 min Fartlek; 15 min regular	Rest	30 min very easy, including stride-outs	Race Day

> ### Be a bit flexible
>
> As I've said before, although these schedules are a good foundation, they are not tablets of stone. This is doubly important now that you're getting hyped up for a race. Everybody's requirements will be slightly different and their capabilities will vary from day to day, so don't be shy about adapting the programmes to suit your specific needs as often as you feel necessary.

increasingly testing events. However, by this point you will know that it's all worth it for the rush of pride when you cross that finish line. Whatever time you did it in…

It's this very personal and entirely direct effort/reward ratio that means entering races can have an effect beyond simply getting you fit. Few other sports push you to compete against yourself in this manner – you don't have to beat anybody, just improve your own performance – or highlight the complete responsibility of the individual inasmuch as, when you're running, there's no hiding behind supposedly dodgy equipment or apparently bone-idle team mates. This is all stuff you can carry over into your life away from running, as once you realize how capable you are of actually pushing yourself to go that extra mile, it won't be nearly so daunting to do it figuratively. Also, the idea that the only performance that really matters is your own will do wonders for your confidence.

Building up to the event

You're not going to win. There, we've said it. Unless you lived a former life as a Kenyan cattle herder who chased his cows, barefoot, at ludicrously high altitudes, it will pretty much be a given that you won't be on the podium at the end of your first race. Chances are you won't come last either, so settle for somewhere in between and look forward to enjoying the event.

> **Fact:** When building up to a race, your weekly mileage, including speed sessions, should be no less than four times the race distance.

However, if you follow our prescribed training schedule you should be pretty certain you'll get round the course, and with the speed work involved you should do so in a time you'll happily admit to. Your focus should be on working up a reserve of strength so that you'll be able to push yourself that little bit harder on race day and finish with a personal best for that distance. This is the ideal conclusion to your race and will give you a tremendous confidence boost to take into your next event.

The schedules you will have been following in the weeks before the race will have been harder than you have been used to – four or five sessions a week instead of three – and that is why tapering off in the couple of weeks before race day is important. You will not be able to perform to your best unless you are sufficiently rested. You have to strike a balance between conserving energy

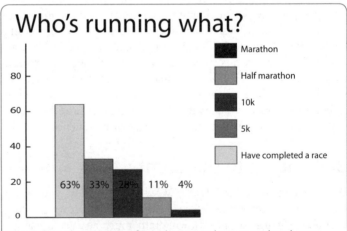

Who's running what?

- Marathon
- Half marathon
- 10k
- 5k
- Have completed a race

63% 33% 28% 11% 4%

These days, the majority of British runners have completed some sort of race. One mile or 2k fun runs are the standard entry point, with 5k and 10k proving particularly popular.

and maintaining the sharpness and speed you have built up in your training, hence reduced speed work during the last couple of weeks of your schedule, and very little of anything in the week before the race. The reason behind this slackening off is that you won't improve much more during that period, and you want to reduce the risk of late injuries as much as possible. During those last few days, any runs you do should be light, and a Fartlek session should keep the emphasis on the "play" rather than the "speed".

What to eat

The fast pace of a 5k or 10k race will burn carbs fairly intensely, but the distance is so short that you shouldn't get anywhere near the bottom of your glycogen reserves, so your regular high-carb eating plan will be enough. You will need to keep those reserves topped off, though, so go in for a carbohydrate stoke-up on the eve of the race. There won't be any desperate need to eat on the morning of the race, but you don't want to feel hungry on the way round either; a couple of pieces of plain toast should suffice, although not within two hours of your start time.

The day before

The idea of going out for an easy run of three or four kilometres on the day before a race is to stay loose and make sure your muscle memory is functioning rather than to actually train. For this reason, make sure you do plenty of stride-outs. Also, it is one of the best things you can do to release a bit of the nervous energy that will be building up. Apart from that, the day before is about rest, relaxation and getting enough to eat. Whether you're doing a 5k or a 10k, have a carb-rich meal in the evening – a big bowl of pasta is ideal, but keep it fairly plain so as not to risk unsettling your stomach. Get all your kit laid out the night before, with your race number secured to

Tip: If you've got a very early start, or you live by yourself, set two alarm clocks, 15 minutes apart. The chances are you'll be awake before either of them, but it's better to be on the safe side.

your top, and pack whatever else you're going to be taking with you. Have some sports drink ready for the next day, but don't start trying to hydrate at this stage or you'll just be getting up in the night.

Plan your timetable for the next morning – it helps to write it down. Work back from your designated start time, and allow an hour between arriving and the gun. Plan the journey and add 25 per cent "sod's law" time, then subtract that from your projected arrival time. Lastly, take off an hour and a half between waking up and leaving the house. This is enough to get you up and out, keeping you moving and occupied, but not so much that you will be sitting about waiting, which wouldn't do you any good at all. Set the alarm for that time, go to bed early and get a good night's sleep.

Race day

Take regular swigs of sports drink from the time you get up, as this will start your hydration process and top up your glycogen levels in an easily metabolized way. Stick to the schedule you prepared

> **❙❙** Concentrate on the task not the outcome. In other words, enjoy the act of running smoothly and with the right level of effort, one mile at a time, rather than your hoped-for results. That will greatly reduce your anxiety levels when it comes to racing. **❙❙**
> **Karen Hancock**

Tip: If you have a timing chip, don't attach it to your shoe before you get to the event. Trains and buses to the bigger races tend to be crowded so it could easily get knocked off and as yours will have been specifically coded to your race number, it cannot be replaced at the start.

Just like rock 'n' roll

When taking part in a race that doesn't supply shirts, it's accepted practice to wear the oldest race shirt you've got, or one from the same event but several years previously. This works along the same principles as laid down for rock fans, when they will wear the oldest tour t-shirt in their wardrobe to that band's concerts – it's a very public statement of commitment to the cause.

the night before: wash, dress, eat and get out of there. If you can possibly avoid it, don't drive yourself to the start – it's unnecessary stress. In fact don't even go in somebody else's car unless you can possibly help it; as many races are on Sundays, there's always a good chance of encountering roadworks that weren't there when you went over the route during the week. Also, driving will be a nightmare even disregarding the extra local traffic, as not only will roads be closed off for the race but all sorts of one-off parking restrictions will be in place.

The hour you allocated at the start will soon pass once you've dropped off your kit bag, found your start area and warmed up. Don't feel at all awkward about going to the toilet as much as you like – all that hydrating and pre-race nerves will inevitably start to take their toll – this is why well-organized races have seemingly excessive numbers of Portaloos on site.

Once the gun goes, for the next thirty or fifty minutes, nobody can give you any advice or tips, and it will all be down to you.

After the race

Once you cross the finish line, collect your medal and keep moving. You may feel like collapsing but don't do it there as there will be a lot more people coming through that very small space. Cool down properly; it will make all the difference later on. Start your rehydration process, but don't be tempted to gulp down litres of water – take it slowly, and try to get some sports drink inside you to start replacing depleted glycogen reserves. Once you get home, enjoy another big bowl of pasta and don't do anything for the rest of the day. You've earned the rest, and you're probably going to want to start plotting your next race.

> **Tip:** There aren't too many tactics to be considered in a 5k race. In fact, once you progress to longer distances you'll treat it as a bit of a sprint! Right from the gun, run at the top end of your regular pace and, if you feel you can still kick it up a bit, go faster again when you hit the final kilometre.

> **Tip:** Don't fixate too much on runners around you who appear to be running at your pace. They might not have your stamina and if they drop off towards the end, you may slow down with them.

> **Fact:** Either through exhilaration or exhaustion or meeting up with their friends, it's very common for inexperienced racers to forget to cool down.

The next day

Have a rest. Although you actually ran less than you've been doing on a regular training day, the intensity of that run and the stress of the whole event will have taken their toll. But only have the one day off. Do the race distance at an easy pace two days after the race then get back to regular training. After all, haven't you got another, longer race to get ready for?

Racing dos and don'ts

✔ Start in your designated slot. These have been allocated so that fast and slow runners aren't tripping over each other when the gun goes off.

✘ If you are running as part of a group don't bunch up causing bottlenecks or run three or four abreast; always be aware of other people trying to pass you.

✔ Always say "Excuse me" or "Coming through" if you have to create some space – don't assume you've been seen.

✔ React quickly to the same from runners coming up behind you.

✔ Remain aware of your fellow racers at all times.

✘ Don't invite friends who haven't entered to run with you – you might be surprised how much of this goes on. There will be reasons why organizers have set the numbers at whatever they are, and going over that will be unfair on and potentially dangerous to other paid-up runners.

✔ Be careful when you throw water cups or bottles away – if you throw it to the side it could hit somebody coming through.

✘ If you have to spit, be extra careful – it's never a bad idea to carry a handkerchief.

Get your mind right

Never forget you'll be racing with your mind almost as much as with your body, and it's important you know how to think your way through those first few races.

At the start

It is far from unusual for novice racers to experience an attack of nerves as they approach the start line – anxieties such as "Have I trained hard enough?", "Is the competition going to be too good?", "Is the course going to be too tough?", "Will I make it?" – that sort of thing. Even the best runners are keyed up before a race, and some of those emotions will involve self-doubt. It's a very rare athlete that *genuinely* has no chink whatsoever in his or her self-confidence – what do you think all those toilets are for?

What it means is that you care – you are worried about your performance and are therefore taking it very seriously. In this respect, anxiety is not only natural but quite an encouraging state of affairs. Unless your pre-match jitters start to affect you physically, simply ride them out, know what they are and take no notice. Then, once the gun goes, there will be no room for them in your thinking.

On the way round

If you're giving your all, whatever distance you're running, at some point you will start to feel wiped out and maybe start to wonder if it's all worth it. In order to keep going, you have to think your way through this patch. You have to remember that fatigue – because that's what it is rather than bonking (see p.242) – comes in waves and will go as suddenly as it hit you. So, think back to times on training runs when you ran through a wave of fatigue with hardly a break in pace.

It's important to be aware that runners who react to this fatigue by feeling depressed and upset by what they perceive to be an inevitable failure of their efforts will probably not get through it. Once these feelings take root they will seem as if they are having a progressive effect. However, those who know it is simply inevitable, and all but celebrate it as a mark of how far they have progressed in the race, will power on through.

At the finish

The chances are, you didn't win the race you've just finished, or maybe you didn't get round in the time you were aiming for, and this can lead to feelings of frustration. It shouldn't do, as this can affect how you will approach your next race or even your future training. Although everybody wants to do well and improve their performance, it can't be done every time and you have to take the positives from every event you take part in.

It can't be stressed strongly enough that just being there and running 26.2 miles round the streets of New York or 5 kilometres along the seafront in Brighton should be the real reason why you're taking part in that race. Unless you're one of the few running elite, all you should be hoping for is a medal, a silver blanket, a smug glow of satisfaction and the respect of your fellow runners. Which ought to be enough.

Ten top runs

There is no shortage of races around the UK for runners of all levels, but here are ten of the country's best that are either big, scenic, interesting or just plain fun.

Great North Run (half marathon, September, Newcastle)

Billed as the world's biggest half marathon, this Tyne and Wear event is part of the BUPA-sponsored Great Run series. Started in 1981, it now attracts 50,000 runners and live BBC TV coverage, and places fill up quickly. **www.greatrun.org**

Brighton Reebok 10k (November)

A fast, flat, relatively easy seafront course. It can be bracing as the wind tends to whip in off the water at this time of the year, but is a good race to record a fast time. Part of the Reebok Premier series of events. **www.brighton-hove.gov.uk**

Nike 10k (September, London)

This enjoyable run is one of the capital's highest-profile participation events and is now so big it has starts both north and south of the Thames. Nike organize training programmes and runs for entrants. **www.runlondon.com**

Flora London Marathon (Spring)

Britain's biggest race has 120,000 entrants for 35,000 places, and so many charity runners in relation to serious athletes that the average finish time has gone up by two hours in the last ten years to more than five hours. **www.london-marathon.co.uk**

Hearts First Santa Dash (three miles, December, Cardiff)

A fun run in every sense of the word, this seasonal South Wales sprint (well, virtually a sprint!), is in aid of the British Heart Foundation and the organizers will even give you a Santa suit to run in! **www.southernwalesevents.co.uk**

Race finder international

Because of the culture of running and the distances involved in the US, Australia and Canada, it is rare for runners to travel too far to any events other than the biggest marathons (unlike in the relatively parochial UK). Thus, it doesn't make sense to list ten top runs for each of those countries and you will be better off checking online for races near you. There are a number of excellent race finder sites across the world featuring continually updated listings for events in that region. Each of these websites has interactive search facilities to help you find your preferred distance, course, date and location:

www.runnersworld.com The site is every bit as comprehensive as its UK counterpart, and in the race finder section you'll find details of every major race in the USA.

www.time-to-run.com/canada On this site the race listings are just part of a service that includes training tips, sports medicine and all-round running advice.

www.coolrunning.com.au The best site down under, it details every big race in categories that go up to Ultramarathon (ie races above 26.2 miles; usually 50 miles, or 52.4 as it's twice the regular marathon distance). It also lists local running clubs.

www.runnersworld.co.uk A comprehensive service from the UK's best-selling running magazine, as part of a website that also offers running news and views, plus a particularly lively forum.

www.fellrunner.org.uk This site specializes in off-road and cross-country events.

www.running.timeoutdoors.com Part of a bigger site that is useful for crosstraining as it also details cycling, walking, climbing and canoeing.

Race For Life (5k, summer, all over the UK)

A series of nationwide women-only 5k runs, taking place in 280 different localities throughout the summer to raise funds for Cancer Research UK. The events are always looking for volunteers to help out on race days. **www.raceforlife.org**

Bupa Great Manchester Run (10k, May)

The biggest running event in the North West's calendar, this 10k loops its way from the city centre to Manchester United's stadium. Part of the Bupa Great Run circuit, it quickly fills its 25,000 entries. **www.greatrun.org**

Hydro Active Women's Challenge (5k, September, Liverpool, Birmingham and London)

A massive women-only 5k event, run simultaneously in London's Hyde Park, Liverpool's Sefton Park and Birmingham City Centre. **www.womenschallenge.co.uk**

Puma Longleat 10k (February, Longleat Safari Park, Wiltshire)

The amount of hills on this race means you won't do a fast time, but so what? Just enjoy the beautiful course around the Marquess of Bath's estate and don't worry, they'll lock up the lions! **www.209events.com**

Run Dunfermline Weekend (Junior 3k, one mile family fun run, 5k, half marathon, last weekend in May)

A festival of running for all ages and abilities taking in the sights of Scotland's ancient capital, with plenty of carnival-style events for non-runners. The half marathon is the climax of two days of different distance runs. **www.dunfermline-half.co.uk**

Age? Nothing but a number

12

I didn't start running seriously until my forties. Did my first marathon at age 44.

Four hours thirty minutes, since you ask.

Although it's probably not such a good idea for previously sedentary 80-year-olds to hurl themselves into an intense running schedule, there aren't many reasons why anybody of any age shouldn't take it up, provided they're fit enough and take a bit of extra care. Similarly, for those who are already running, carrying on into your second half century shouldn't be a problem, although you might have to adjust your expectations a wee bit. This chapter discusses how to do both.

70 can be the new 30

I know people in Florida who are twenty years older than me and still turn in times of around four hours for marathons. In that heat!

They could strip paint with the looks of contempt they summon up when somebody asks them "You don't still run, do you?". Indeed, the thing that struck me most about the first London Marathon I took part in was how much older the field was than for the shorter races I had been entering – two or three times I had been the oldest runner in 10k events, yet lining up at the start of the marathon I was definitely one of the kids.

At the time of writing, the world record for a septuagenarian's marathon stands at 2 hours 54 minutes 49 seconds, set by Canada-dwelling Brit Ed Whitlock. It's a time that would put him in the top one or two per cent of finishers in the world's major marathons, yet would still be nearly an hour behind the winners. This deftly illustrates two points about senior running: at age 73 he was able to set the sort of pace most of us youngsters can only dream about (an average 6.67 minute mile – *over 26.2 of them*); and in an overall context, even such a stellar performance is relatively slow.

For the retiree, running is the ideal activity: quite apart from the physical and mental benefits, you have time to work to interesting training schedules and enter far-flung events

Although it's possible to run very fast at an advanced age, there's no way you're going to run as fast as a thirty-year-old, and it could be as dangerous as it will be frustrating to even attempt to do so. However, the good news is that, with a regular running programme, even those seventy-year-olds who might not set any records can achieve the levels of cardiovascular fitness of somebody forty years younger. This is due to the size and efficiency of their hearts compared with their sedentary counterparts. As part of the aging process the heart will naturally get smaller, stiffer and weaker; regular running keeps it working above "normal" levels to maintain strength and flexibility. Tests at the University of Texas involving resting and running heart rates and VO_2 max (see pp.111–112) showed the hearts of a group of runners with an average age of seventy to be "indistinguishable from healthy thirty-year-olds". Another US survey compared fifty-something runners of both sexes to inactive men and women in their twenties, and found both groups to have the same VO_2 maximals.

> **Tip:** Older runners will benefit considerably from running on softer surfaces because it is so much kinder on the knees and ankles. Rugged cross-country is not such a good idea because of the increased likelihood of falls and stumbles.

Slowly does it

Seniors coming into running for the first time will need to follow fairly strict guidelines. They will naturally have suffered a degree of muscle mass wastage so they have to make sure they are strong enough to run. For those who have lived a more sedentary lifestyle, this will mean a schedule of walking before starting to run. Atrophied muscles will need to be developed to the point where they can power the limbs sufficiently for running and will be strong enough to support and protect the joints. Walking will also start to raise cardiovascular levels and decrease both working and resting heart rates to the point at which running becomes safe and much easier.

A heart-rate monitor will be a vital piece of kit, because measuring your

> **Fact:** Older runners spend much longer than their younger counterparts in the stance phase of a stride, dampening any explosive action and so greatly reducing their speed.

> **Tip:** To improve speeds, older runners should concentrate on their stride length, as it declines fairly rapidly after the age of 45 whereas stride frequency hardly changes at all.

Getting over it

Recovery time for an older runner will be significantly greater as your body will regenerate at a much slower rate. Leave at least 48 hours between your runs, and on potential running days take your pulse as soon as you get up – if it is higher than your normal resting rate, you have not fully recovered from your last run and another day off should be on the cards.

Fact: A 21-year study in Finland found the incidence of regular runners suffering hip problems to be half the national average – four per cent as opposed to eight.

Overtraining alert!

Only carry on running for as long as you can do so in the correct style. As soon as your form gets sloppy, pack it in for the day because it means you are getting tired.

pulse is the key to any initial programme, as it will determine the speed and duration of your preparatory walks. Strap it on, note your resting heart rate then determine your maximum by taking a brisk walk round the block and make a note of that too. Your schedule will then consist of walking three times a week for between twenty and thirty minutes, maintaining 75 per cent of your maximum rate. Record resting and exercising figures every day and after a month you should have noticed a significant drop in both, indicating your aerobic capacity is increasing. After two months, your heart rates should have continued to fall as you will have been building up muscle strength and you ought to be ready to take on the first phase training schedule (see p.18).

Run for your life

In an eight-year study at Stanford University of 538 runners (some of whom had never run before) and 423 non-runners, all aged between 50 and 72, the runners were four times less likely to experience disabilities related to their muscular and skeletal systems. The runners made a third as many visits to medical facilities as non-runners, missed half as many days at work through sickness and had lower blood pressure. The non-runners were five times more likely to suffer knee and ankle problems and, astonishingly, twenty times more likely to have trouble with arms and shoulders. Forty per cent of the runners suffered a running-related injury, but that would hold true for any group of runners. However, only eight had to completely give up running through injury. During the length of the survey, thirty non-runners died compared with eight of the runners.

Scaling back

Long-time runners should be listening to their bodies as the years roll by, and as well as increasing recovery time (see box top left) they should be naturally easing off on their target times, paces and training schedules. How much these need to be reduced depends entirely on the individual, but it isn't unreasonable to expect a reduction of six to eight per cent in your performance each year once you pass sixty.

Eating and drinking

Just like anybody taking on a new programme of exercise, older runners will need to adjust their diet to increase carbohydrates intake and cut down on fat (see pp.30–33), as a running metabolism doesn't really care how old the runner is.

You may need to address your protein intake, though, and make sure it is high enough – the appetite for protein tends to decrease with the passing of the years because less is required and a reduction in stomach acid makes digesting red meat a much longer process. For the latter reason, you may find it easier to switch to vegetable protein from foods like beans, lentils and nuts.

Dehydration can be a particular problem past the age of fifty – you will lose fluid faster on your run because your optimum body temperature will be higher than a younger person's, while your thirst sensors will be less sensitive than they used to be. So be very aware of dehydration, as you will need more fluid but be less aware of it.

Fact: As an effect of the aging process men lose their muscle mass twice as fast as women.

Tip: Be careful of old, long-forgotten injuries resurfacing once you start running. If they persist, seek medical advice.

Tip: Never forget you are doing this to benefit yourself – for fun and fitness. Don't let it become a chore, a pain (literally) or a frustration; leave competitiveness to the youngsters and run for your own pleasure.

Tip: Non-impact activities such as swimming or cycling are best for seniors suffering from pre-existing joint or bone problems.

Be prepared to learn

Don't be surprised if, once you start, running has to be a conscious rather than an unconscious action as your motor neuron system may well have forgotten how to run. You'll need to learn how to run again by reprogramming the pathways that get your legs and arms pumping without you having to think about it. For this reason stride-outs and other running style skills rehearsals should be a big part of your early training. Also, pay careful attention to stretching and flexibility exercises, which will allow you to perform these now unfamiliar actions with less internal resistance.

Weight in the wings

There is no reason at all why seniors can't supplement their running with weight training. Indeed, it's an ideal non-impact way to strengthen muscles in preparation for running. You should opt for higher repetitions of lighter weights, which ought to mean lifting not much more than a bag of shopping – the only difference is you'll be doing it more often and with different muscles.

Tip: Don't be shy about going for a run. I promise, nobody will be staring at you with anything other than respect and admiration.

Age-related racing

For nearly twenty years there has been a system in operation that allows runners to adjust their timings according to age and gender. Known as Age Grading, it was developed in 1989 by the World Association of Veteran Athletes, the governing body for senior running, and it works by taking the world record over that distance for athletes of that age and gender, and dividing it by your time, to give an answer measured as a percentage. For instance, let's assume I run a 10k in forty minutes. Because the world record for 52-year-old men is 31 minutes 1.2 seconds, I divide that by my time to give an answer of 0.78. This means my age-graded result for that distance would be 78 per cent. Results in a race would then be figured by which runner had the highest age-graded number, regardless of actual timings.

As the world's running population gets older, age grading is becoming increasing popular in clubs and at many major events, with the "age-related champions" over the various distances being awarded trophies alongside the outright winners.

www.runningforfitness.org/faq/agegrading.php has an interactive calculator to work out your age-graded performances, and a reverse facility to tell you what times you need to be running to achieve target grading percentages.

The great osteoporosis myth

It used to be considered wisdom that those of us of a certain age shouldn't run for fear of bringing on the sort of bone and joint damage connected with osteoporosis or arthritis. Recent research has shown precisely the opposite to be true. Although it is not recommended for anybody suffering either of those conditions to take up running without first seeking medical advice, for the rest of us running is one of the best measures you can take against them.

Regular running strengthens the muscles and connective tissues that support bones and joints, meaning everyday stresses will be greatly reduced. The flexibility gained through stretching and the running motion will ease joint stiffness and help regain a range of movement you might have thought consigned to history. Running significantly reduces the likelihood of osteoarthritis, too, as it strengthens the cartilage and increases production of synovial fluid to lubricate joints and lessen wear through friction. Runners' bones will have greater density as well, and they will suffer less natural mineral loss because the body will have adapted itself to cope with the rigours of the road. It is, however, a very good idea for the older end of senior runners (seventy-plus) to take calcium supplements to ensure this bone density is maintained.

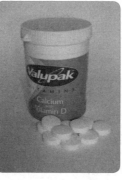

Be warned, though, that cartilage wear is cumulative and no matter how careful you have been it will eventually go and you'll have to take up swimming. One of the reasons Ed Whitlock is still running at his level is because he didn't run a step between the ages of 21 and 41, meaning he has the knees of a man twenty years his junior.

Fact: Of the "wear and tear" on the joints, it's the tearing that presents the much greater problem. Sports such as football or basketball that involve a great deal of stop-starting and twisting do much more damage than running's constant forward motion.

> Running is probably the best cardiovascular exercise of the lot for seniors. Just make sure you have the best shoes available to reduce the impact on articular cartilage (the cartilage covering bones in joints) and try to run on grass wherever possible. I used to train through the woods on Hampstead Heath where centuries of leaf mould produced the ideal springy surface to soften the blows.
> **Barrie Savory D.O.**

Girl power!

It's difficult to imagine, but it was only thirty years ago that women took up running in large numbers…

And it's been less than 25 years since the Olympics included a women's marathon. Yet for the last decade women in their twenties have been the fastest growing runners' demographic.

The great thing about this last point is that, unlike with tennis, football or squash, most men and women can run together on a fairly equal basis as, below the elite level, there's hardly any difference between what they can achieve and how they need to train for it. However, there are some aspects of running that affect women uniquely, and this chapter will deal with them.

Increase the iron

Iron deficiency is common among women, who need almost twice the RDA of men yet in general eat less. Plus, the iron turnover among distance runners is higher than for other athletes. Therefore, women runners need much more iron – 18mg per day and, especially if they are vegetarian, this may mean taking supplements.

Tip: Surprisingly, to combat premenstrual bloating you should actually drink more water. Bloating is triggered by sodium retention, but increased fluid and sweating while running will flush it out.

Running through the month

Gone are the days when girls on their periods were made to sit out of PE – at the 2004 Olympics in Athens, one third of all women's gold medals were won by menstruating athletes. Most female runners will carry on throughout their period and, although there are no hard and fast rules as no two women runners are the same, most discomfort is reported in the premenstrual and first-flow days. On the upside, however, many women find the "runner's high" of endorphins flooding the brain will alleviate premenstrual syndrome, while the physical act of running eases period pains. Women runners also maintain that running's general lifting of the spirits goes a long way towards counteracting the physiological changes that are happening. Sweating profusely can also reduce bloating by clearing the system of excess sodium (see box below left).

The motion of running will affect all women differently as regards blood flow, but for most running with sanitary wear needn't be too much of a problem. Thicker towels and pads can bunch up, so choose the thinnest available, with wings. A significant proportion of women are worried about full tampons leaking while running, and will wear a pad as well. Whatever you use, change it before and after running, and be aware that you will need to wear underwear, even with shorts or tights that don't usually require it.

Keep a diary

To understand how your training schedule and your menstrual cycle affect each other, keep a diary or notes in your training log of how you ran, how you felt and how your body reacted. If a physiological pattern emerges over several months, you can use that to determine when you should race or how to get the most out of your training. However, adjusting or stopping your periods to fit in with a race schedule is not recommended.

Physical differences (apart from the obvious)

Timings for female athletes, over all distances, will be around ten per cent slower than those of similarly trained men. This is mainly due to three reasons:

1) Even after training and conditioning, women retain a higher percentage of body fat and have a lower muscle-to-weight ratio than men, so less has to carry more.

2) Women's hearts and arteries are proportionately smaller and therefore have to work harder.

3) They also have proportionately lower haemoglobin levels than men, which means that even more effort is needed from that smaller heart to deliver enough oxygen to the muscles.

The good news is that once women start training, they tend to get fitter more quickly than men, and register greater relative improvements.

Female athlete triad syndrome

This is the term for a worryingly increasing condition among hard-training women that consists of three interlinked disorders – amenorrhoea, anorexia and osteoporosis. This is more common among adolescent athletes as their understanding of their body and their metabolism hasn't had the benefit of a great deal of experience in either life or running.

Fact: Women in their premenstrual phase are more likely to suffer running injuries. This is believed to be because the temporary hormonal imbalance affects the motor neuron pathways.

Exercise-related amenorrhoea

Consistent intense training has been shown to bring on amenorrhoea, the cessation of the menstrual cycle. Although

// Running while pregnant is going to be different for everybody. During my last pregnancy it was very difficult during the last third because of the straightforward problems of running with a large lump in front of you, and the difficulty there is in breathing properly. I did a lot of walking instead. //
Karen Hancock

// More important than running through a pregnancy is getting back to running soon afterwards. As a runner you'll need to get that personal time back because it's become an important part of your life, and getting back to health and fitness will also be important. Plus it's a good way to lose weight. //
Karen Hancock

research is ongoing and nothing conclusive has yet been established, the causes are believed to be an over-production of endorphins and catecholamines affecting the balance of oestrogen and progesterone, or very low body weight. If you suffer from this for several months, scale back on your training and seek medical advice.

Oestrogen, heavy training and osteoporosis

Although an activity such as running promotes good bone density, the hormone oestrogen is essential for maintaining healthy bones. Amenorrhoea can mean drastically reduced levels of oestrogen, counteracting running's beneficial effects and greatly increasing the risks of stress fractures or osteoporosis. The same also applies to post-menopausal runners. There has been a move, more in the US than the UK, for doctors to treat this by prescribing the contraceptive pill to raise oestrogen levels and control cycles. Many women don't agree with this treatment, and find the bone-building supplements calcium and vitamin D to be just as effective.

Anorexia

Despite the emphasis on eating properly and an assumed understanding of how calorific metabolism actually works, anorexia is not uncommon among aspiring female athletes, distance runners in particular. This is despite the fact that their performances will be the most acutely affected by an unsuitable or inadequate diet. As discussed earlier, endurance athletes' bodies will always let them know what they need, and under these circumstances the runner concerned has to make sure she listens.

Pregnant pauses

If you already run there is no reason why you can't continue into your pregnancy for as long as you feel totally comfortable. However, it would not be advisable to take up running while pregnant. Initially, your two biggest worries will be dehydration and overheating; if your core temperature gets too high it could damage the foetus, while dehydration could result in reduced blood flow to the uterus causing contractions to start. Drink plenty of water, perhaps more than you might usually.

As your pregnancy progresses, your joints will loosen which can increase the risk of falling, or twisting your knees or ankles. Also, as your bump grows, so your centre of gravity will shift and it will be necessary to adjust your running posture to maintain correct balance. It is advisable to shift to a more even, softer surface – track running is ideal for expectant runners, with the bonus that you will not be alone in case something does go wrong.

During the final months, take it easy. Never run to the point of exhaustion or even breathlessness because you will be diverting oxygen away from your baby in order to keep your muscles moving. Slow your pace down, indeed you may find brisk walking more suitable, and if you feel like taking a day off from running do so without feeling guilty.

> *The biggest danger of running when you're pregnant is overheating. It can happen without you realizing it, and too big a rise in your core temperature can be very hazardous to your baby.*
> **Efua Baker**

> *Running during a pregnancy is a good way to keep your blood pressure down, but only do it for as long as you feel comfortable.*
> **Karen Hancock**

Stop running immediately if you experience any of the following:

Vaginal bleeding or fluid leaking

Drastic shortness of breath

Contractions

Exhaustion

Uncomfortable rise in body temperature

Dizziness

Chest pains

Tip: If you are running during pregnancy you will need extra support, so make sure your shoes are in top condition or invest in a new, more stable pair. If your bump isn't showing yet, make sure you tell the salespersons you are expecting.

C-section

If you've had a Caesarean section or any stitches, make sure you get clearance from your midwife before getting back on the road.

Fact: Know that 99.9999 per cent of all male runners will never run as fast as Paula Radcliffe.

Chest expansions

Because breasts are mostly fatty tissue they will have reduced in size when you started running. With pregnancy, though, they will grow considerably and support will become an issue. Previously women runners sometimes resorted to wearing two bras, but now a large range of specialist maternity sports bras are available – check out **www.boobydoo.co.uk** for a large selection. Pectoral strengthening exercises – bench presses and press ups with your hands set slightly further apart – are also recommended for internal support and the apparent firming of the bust.

After the birth

If you are fit and healthy, you will recover from the rigours of childbirth more efficiently, thus you can get back to running as soon as you feel ready. Once again, listen to your body and start gently – perhaps just walking – working back gradually to easy running (see pp.65–66). Don't push yourself too hard because losing weight too quickly at this time isn't ideal, and producing large amounts of lactic acid can affect the taste of your milk – although it won't do your baby any harm, they simply might not like it. Go running right after you have fed your baby, as this will minimize discomfort, lessen the likelihood of leakage and baby will be less likely to make a fuss while you are out. It is also very important to stay hydrated so as to not to hinder your milk production.

The big 26.2

On the surface of it, leaving your house to run for four or five hours is ridiculous.

In that time, other people have watched a double bill at the cinema, ridden Eurostar to Paris, been to two football matches, done half a day in the office, learned most of a foreign language... and you're still running. But so many people are running marathons these days that the last London Marathon could have filled each one of its 30,000-plus places four times over. This chapter looks at what a marathon is, how much it can take out of your body, and why it won't be so hard for you to run one.

A right royal distance

The marathon wasn't always 26.2 miles. In fact the original, legendary marathon, run in 490 BC, wasn't even 26 miles. Myth has it that after the heavily outnumbered Athenian army had defeated the Persians at the Battle of Marathon, Phidippides, a foot soldier, ran the entire 24 miles back to the Greek capital to announce "Rejoice. We are victorious!" before he dropped dead from exhaustion. Note the distance.

For the 1896 Athens Olympics, the last Games of the nineteenth century and the first of the modern era, it was decided to mark the event and the venue with a 40k (24.8 mile) race, named the marathon. A regular of the Games since then, it varied in distance from 40 to nearly 43 kilometres (24.8 to 26.56 miles) depending on where the course had been marked out – all that mattered was that it was a very long way and all runners ran the same course.

As part of the 1908 London Olympics, the marathon was scheduled at precisely 26 miles, starting in the grounds of Windsor Castle and finishing in the White City Stadium in West London (now the site of a BBC building). King Edward VII, then in residence at the Castle, wanted to start the race, but had a cold and on doctor's orders wasn't allowed out into the grounds. Thus the start was moved 385 yards up the hill so it could happen in

Imperial alert!

Because marathons and half marathons are measured in miles and the course is marked off in miles, traditionally so too are the training runs. Therefore, virtually any conversation you have about the races will be conducted in fluent Imperial. If you want a translation into modern-day English, multiply miles by 1.609 to get kilometres; divide by the same figure to go the other way.

the Castle's courtyard and His Majesty could do the honours. The finish line, however, couldn't be moved at it had to be in line with the royal box, where his wife Queen Alexandria was sitting, meaning the length of that marathon was 26 miles 385 yards, or 26.218 miles.

Although the Olympic marathon distance changed distance twice for the next two Games, in 1909 the Polytechnic Marathon was run over that same 26.218 mile Windsor to White City route and immediately established itself as an annual event. The race gained such prestige that in 1924 the International Association of Athletics Federations (IAAF) adopted the distance as an international standard, rounding it up to up to 26.22 miles.

> // Most runners that do a marathon do one and that's it, they never do another. That's because while it's definitely an attainable goal, it won't suit everybody, so in most cases it will make more sense to run shorter distances. //
> **Hugh Jones**

But some are more equal than others

Although all marathons are now the same length, the effort involved can vary enormously depending on temperatures, elevation and how flat the course is. This is why records tend to get broken far more frequently in some cities (Chicago and London, for instance) than in others, and old hands will advise that certain marathons (New York) shouldn't be attempted by novices.

Marathon psychology

The first few miles of a marathon are in your head, and have to be conquered months before the starting line. Because most runners see the marathon as the Holy Grail, it has an often-overwhelming stigma attached to it. Indeed, it's not unusual for runners to divide themselves into two categories, "Those who have run a marathon" and "Those who haven't", and take the approach that you're somehow not quite a "proper" runner unless you've done one.

Don't rush into it

It's not a good idea for new runners to jump straight into a marathon training schedule. Because of both the physical and mental strength required, you should have at least a year's distance running experience first to fully understand how your body reacts to it.

Pace expectations

To roughly – and I do mean roughly – predict what speed you should be running a marathon at, follow this easy formula. Divide your 10k minutes-per-kilometre pace by 0.88, multiply the answer by 42.2 and divide that result by 26.2. This tells you what your minutes-per-mile pace ought roughly to be. This formula also works with your 5k pace (divide by 0.85) or your half marathon pace (divide by 0.95).

Tip: Write your name in large letters on your running top and the crowds lining the route will cheer you on personally, which always provides a massive boost.

> When I ran my first marathon I was very much aware that it was an experiment, and I had no idea if I was going to be any good at it, then it turned out to be the distance I was best at. Approach every new distance with an open mind.
>
> **Hugh Jones**

Such a state of affairs is, of course, utter nonsense, much like that ludicrous debate of running vs jogging. *Anyone* who runs regularly is a proper runner, and don't let anybody tell you otherwise – less than ten per cent of all recreational runners will ever finish a marathon, so how can the vast majority be bogus? However, the race's exalted status also means that every runner who decides to run a marathon won't have taken that decision lightly. And that's where the psychology begins.

Training your mind

Because running 26.2 miles is such unnatural behaviour, you will have to think yourself into it before you even start to plan a training schedule, and this in itself can be a stumbling block for many potential marathoners. Because of the sheer size of marathon mythology few runners, even those with decent 10k times, assume

Teamwork

When you're taking that initial decision to run a marathon, get together with some friends and do it as a bunch. You'll work to convince each other you can do it and training will be more enjoyable. Run it as a team too, so you can continue to support each other. Do it in matching gear and you'll be guaranteed a good response from spectators as you run.

they could do one, thus they need to talk themselves into it. And about fifty per cent will end up talking themselves out of it.

Once you've made the decision that such a feat could be possible, the first long training runs put up another mental barrier; as you move out of your comfort zone – by some distance – it's like starting all over again and all those "Can I do it?" and "Is it worth it?" questions pop up. But, just like when you started running and you felt like that first 5k was the outer limit, you'll push on and those fifteen and twenty milers will seem like nothing in a few weeks' time. It is important to keep this in mind, as marathon training is a six-month stretch of perpetually moving out of your comfort zone and there will be times when you'll need all your mental strength to carry on with it.

Race day psychology

After what you've been through in the past months, race day psychology is relatively straightforward. After all, if you've trained correctly you'll know you can do it and you've had all the time since your entry was accepted to be thinking about it. On the day you'll be swept along by the other runners and the cheering crowds, thus your only concern during the first nineteen or twenty miles should be enjoying the day.

If you've never run 26.2 miles before, you will be astonished at how much longer it seems than your twenty mile training runs. This is because you've hit the wall (see p.240), and as you switch from burning glycogen to burning mainly fat everything will become much more difficult.

Your pace will slow, you'll want to quit and it's going take a supreme act of willpower to keep going. But on average more than two-thirds of those who started the race will finish it, and there's no reason why you can't be one of them.

Tip: If your pace starts to slow don't worry too much, make a calculation, adjust your expectations and go for a new goal.

// Running 26-plus miles on hard, unforgiving tarmac is quite a task for the body. The limb joints, ankles, knees and hips bear the brunt of this stress. The biggest problem comes towards the end of the race when tired muscles make you lose the spring in your stride and you thump down more heavily. This is when impact damage occurs to the articular surfaces (the bits of the joints that rub against each other). Make sure you have the best shock-absorbing shoes that you can buy. //
Barrie Savory D.O.

Tip: Make sure you include stride-outs in your shorter runs as with the distances you are going to put in you could waste a great deal of energy with incorrect technique.

The wall – and how to get around it

There's a good reason why it's called the wall. At about the nineteen or twenty mile marker, without warning, a runner will experience such dramatic fatigue that it is likened to running into a brick wall. Your legs seem to weigh a ton each, as if you suddenly have no energy whatsoever. Which is pretty much what has actually happened as your body has burned off its glycogen reserves.

Most people can store enough glycogen in their muscles and liver to run for between eighteen and twenty miles, burning a cocktail of approximately 75 per cent glycogen and 25 per cent fat. After the glycogen is burned off the fuel supply becomes pure fat, which burns far less easily and, because it requires much more oxygen to burn properly, is not nearly as efficient a fuel as glycogen. Furthermore, fat burning requires a small amount of glycogen as a catalyst, and if there isn't any glycogen, the fat can't burn at all. Hence the abrupt loss of energy.

> **In an average marathon, sixty per cent of non-elite runners will hit the wall, but that also means forty per cent won't. So it is avoidable.**

To get past the wall for those remaining few miles, you will need to improve your glycogen-storing capacity, burn it at as slow a rate as possible and take on carbohydrates earlier in the race. Long training runs of more than fifteen miles over a six-month period will naturally build up your glycogen capacity, while carb loading (see p.242) can greatly increase the amount of glycogen in your muscles on race day.

You can effectively manage your glycogen consumption in order to conserve those stores. The more energy you have to put into your running, the more glycogen in proportion to fat you will burn for each stride – the 75/25 ratio is for an easy pace – so being properly

Don't go mad

Overtraining can be very common among those training for their first marathon, and you should be wary of doing more than forty miles per week. Also, if you suffer any impact-related injuries, break from your running schedule and cross train until it has fully recovered, as the sort of distances you're doing now could seriously aggravate it.

It's not easy, but it's far from impossible

If you can run 10k you can run a marathon. At least that's what my fitness instructor told me almost ten years ago and I fell for it. His logic was that once you understood the principles of distance running training – increasing your duration, upping you VO$_2$ max and doing speed sessions – applying it to a marathon was no different from a 10k, there was just more of it. He had a point, too.

Training for a marathon isn't so complicated, it's simply a matter of making sure you have long enough to prepare for it – at least six months if you're coming at it as a regular 10k runner – and a high enough level of both basic and running fitness to cope with the stresses of marathon training. Basic fitness is measured as your VO$_2$ max (see p.111), while running fitness is vital to build up the muscle and tendon strength and the resistance to impact in your bones and joints that you're going to need to run 26.2 miles.

You will need to train three or four times a week, including one long run, which is just plain running with at least one rest day after it. Shorter runs should contain speed work, intervals and Fartlek. Work the distances of your long runs up on a fortnightly basis, increasing by about twelve per cent a month leading up to twenty-mile runs by a month before the race. Then you need to start tapering off, reducing by ten per cent per week. Your final long run – twelve miles or more – should be no less than ten days before race day, and you should rest up completely in the two or three days prior, with maybe a loosening jog with some stride-outs the afternoon before. The minimum level you should have reached is to be able to run for four hours without huge discomfort – the Flora London Marathon asks that you defer your place until the following year if you are not capable of running fifteen miles.

trained will allow you to run at a decent clip without pushing yourself too hard. Also, avoid the common beginner's mistake of trying to "bank" mileage by starting off at too fast a pace, as you will be burning glycogen too quickly and too soon. Experienced marathoners run the first couple of miles at a minute or so below their regular race pace then step it up a gear, and this energy saved will repay in about nineteen miles' time.

The most straightforward method is to take on board easily metabolized calories during the run, as these will renew your glycogen supplies. These can be in the form of sports drinks or high-calorie energy food, and should be consumed every half an hour after the first hour of running – a feature of all big marathons is generous spectators holding out trays of chocolate or banana pieces throughout the route.

Carb loading

The average trained athlete stores between 1500 and 1900 calories of glycogen, around seventy per cent in the muscles and thirty per cent in the liver. Carb loading, done correctly, can increase these amounts by as much as ninety per cent.

The most commonly used method starts one week before race day with an intense but not exhaustive run of at least an hour to deplete your glycogen stores. Then, during the next three days, continue

Oi lardy!

If you want to improve your performance in a marathon, lose some weight. Runners spend small fortunes on lightweight kit hoping to save a gram or so, but will still run carrying ten kilograms of dead weight in the form of excess body fat. Don't try to do it with a crash diet just before race day, though, or you'll leave yourself weakened.

with your sixty per cent carbohydrate diet and train lightly. In the three days before the race, increase your carb intake to 75 per cent, cutting back on fat and protein to maintain the same amount of calories; stop training and rest during this time. Because each gram of carbohydrate you take on is accompanied by four grams of water, this carb-fest may leave you feeling a bit bloated – don't worry, this extra water will be put to good use once you start running.

Then there is the Western Australia Method, developed during the first years of this millennium and named after its university of origin. It is an intense combination of depletion and splurging that takes place in a 24-hour time frame and can boost glycogen storage again by as much as ninety per cent.

During the week before the race follow your sixty per cent carb diet and train lightly – the Western Australia Method works best at the end of a taper. On the morning of the day before the race, perform a very brief (five minutes), highly intense (130 per cent of VO₂ max) series of thirty-second sprints, then over the next 24 hours eat twelve grams of carbohydrate for every 45 grams (lb) of body weight. The easiness of the training during the week makes sure glycogen levels remain high, while this short intense burst of exercise is sufficient to stimulate over-compensation during the coming 24 hours, without tiring you out before a marathon.

In each case, glycogen levels should be topped up just before the race with a sports drink or a piece of fruit.

Tip: If you're already doing half marathons, you could work up to the whole thing in three months. Otherwise, take half a year to prepare.

// It's after a marathon that ice will really come into its own as it will help to minimize the damage by stimulating the circulation of blood.
Barrie Savory D.O.

Fact: Carb loading was developed in the 1960s by Swedish physiologist Gunvar Ahlborg, who discovered that if you starved the body of glycogen for several days, then binged on carbohydrate for the next few days, your system would over-compensate and store abnormally high amounts. During the next decade it was discovered that the binge itself was enough and you didn't need the depletion.

Half marathon training schedule

Tip: If you have limited training hours, leave out the speed sessions to concentrate on endurance training.

This assumes you are starting from a level where you're running thirty to forty miles a week, can run a 10k in less than an hour, and are fit enough to run four or five days a week.

Week	Monday	Tuesday	Wednesday	Thursday	Friday	Saturday	Sunday
One	Rest	6 miles	Rest	5 miles including Fartlek	Rest	4 miles	8 miles
Two	Rest	6 miles including hills	Rest	6 miles	Rest	4 miles	9 miles
Three	Rest	6 miles including Fartlek	5 miles	6 miles	Rest	4 miles	10 miles
Four	Rest	6 miles	8 miles	6 miles including intervals	Rest	4 miles	10k at race pace
Five	Rest	6 miles, 3 of them at 5k race pace	7 miles	8 miles	Rest	4 miles	9 miles
Six	Rest	8 miles including hills	8 miles	8 miles	Rest	4 miles	11 miles
Seven	Rest	6 miles including intervals	7 miles	9 miles	Rest	3 miles	15k at race pace
Eight	Rest	9 miles, 4 of them at 5k race pace	7 miles	8 miles	Rest	4 miles	12 miles
Nine	Rest	8 miles including hills	8 miles	8 miles	Rest	4 miles	13 miles
Ten	Rest	6 miles, 3 of them at 5k race pace	9 miles	8 miles	Rest	3 miles	15 miles
Eleven	Rest	6 miles including intervals	Rest	7 miles	Rest	4 miles	8 miles
Twelve	Rest	6 miles	4 miles	Rest	Rest	3 miles including stride-outs	Race Day

Marathon training schedule

This programme assumes you are of a standard to have completed a half marathon in a respectable time (under two hours), and are running 35 to 40 miles a week. The mileage will not go above forty miles per week very often, because any benefit at that point becomes relatively much less and the chance of injury much greater. It also includes crosstraining (select your own exercise, see pp.131–133) to keep your VO$_2$ levels up but reduce the cumulative stress of running.

> Use prescribed schedules as a framework or guideline rather than a precise recipe. They have to be fairly general, meaning there's a good chance they won't be right for you without some sort of adjustments, so don't fixate on what is written down.
> **Karen Hancock**

Week	Monday	Tuesday	Wednesday	Thursday	Friday	Saturday	Sunday
One	Rest	5 miles Fartlek	7 miles	Rest	Cross train 1 hour	6 miles	12 miles
Two	Rest	8 miles	6 miles including hills	Rest	Cross train 1 hour	6 miles	15 miles
Three	Rest	9 miles	Rest	5 miles at 5k pace	Cross train 1 hour	8 miles	16 miles
Four	Rest	5 miles Fartlek	10 miles	10 miles	Cross train 1 hour	6 miles	Half marathon
Five	Rest	8 miles	8 miles, 4 of them at 5k pace	Rest	Cross train 1 hour	7 miles	12 miles
Six	Rest	9 miles	5 miles Fartlek	Rest	Cross train 1 hour	7 miles	15 miles
Seven	Rest	8 miles	Rest	6 miles including hills	Cross train 1 hour	6 miles	18 miles
Eight	Rest	8 miles including intervals	8 miles	Rest	Cross train 1 hour	6 miles	18 miles
Nine	Rest	10 miles	8 miles, 4 of them at 5k pace	Rest	Cross train 1 hour	8 miles	14 miles
Ten	Rest	8 miles	Rest	5 miles Fartlek	Cross train 1 hour	6 miles	20 miles

Marathon training schedule (continued)

Week	Monday	Tuesday	Wednesday	Thursday	Friday	Saturday	Sunday
Eleven	Rest	8 miles	8 miles including hills	Rest	Cross train 1 hour	7 miles	16 miles
Twelve	Rest	10 miles	Rest	8 miles, 4 of them at 5k pace	Cross train 1 hour	7 miles	Half marathon at race pace
Thirteen	Rest	6 miles Fartlek	Rest	9 miles	Cross train 1 hour	7 miles	18 miles
Fourteen	Rest	10 miles	6 miles including hills	Rest	Cross train 1 hour	7 miles	20 miles
Fifteen	Rest	8 miles	8 miles, 4 of them at 5k pace	Rest	Cross train 1 hour	7 miles	22 miles
Sixteen	Rest	6 miles including intervals	Rest	8 miles	Cross train 1 hour	6 miles	24 miles
Seventeen	Rest	8 miles	6 miles including intervals	Rest	Cross train 1 hour	5 miles including stride-outs	Marathon
Eighteen	Rest	6 miles including hills	Rest	8 miles	Cross train 45 mins	7 miles	14 miles
Nineteen	Rest	8 miles	6 miles	Rest	Cross train 30 mins	6 miles	8 miles
Twenty	Rest	4 miles	4 miles	Rest	Rest	3 miles including stride-outs	Race Day

Ten top marathons

Proving there is life in the international marathon circuit beyond the popular races in London (**www.london-marathon.co.uk**) and New York (**www.ingnycmarathon.org**), here are ten races worth checking out.

North Pole

April, 110 runners have completed the five races so far

The world's coolest marathon is run entirely on the frozen Arctic ocean, and in spite of the extreme conditions, organizers maintain any marathon runner can do it provided they dress warmly enough. The £12,000 ($20,000) entry fee might prove prohibitive, though, but that does include transport from Norway, accommodation and the chance to stand at the actual Geographic North Pole.

www.npmarathon.com

Boston

April, 20,000 runners

The world's oldest annual marathon has been going since 1897 and is not for the average charity runner. Quite apart from the hill on the course, entry qualification involves having run a fairly fast time within the 18 months before the race – for instance men aged between 35 and 39 must run below 3 hours 15 min, and women aged between 18 and 34 must run below 3 hours 40 min.

www.bostonmarathon.org

Great Wall of China

May, 700 runners

This tough course – mostly uphill and with 3,700 steps – takes in some breathtaking scenery as it passes through villages and

10 tips for international racing

1. Pack your running shoes in your carry-on luggage, as these are the one thing you don't want to be separated from.

2. Make sure you haven't remained dehydrated from your flight.

3. Take cold water washing powder/liquid with you so you can wash your kit in your hotel room.

4. Do your best to stay awake until the local bedtime, then try to sleep until the right time, locally, to get up.

5. If you can't arrive early enough to get used to a different time, adjust your sleeping patterns before you travel.

6. Expose yourself to as much natural daylight as possible – it will help you beat jet lag.

7. Be certain to find out if there is a local registration you need to attend before you get your race number.

8. If you're in your new location several days before your race, make sure you don't wear yourself out doing the tourist thing.

9. Find a good pasta restaurant! Race organizers might have a list of suitable candidates.

10. Travel the journey from your hotel to the start before race day. Then allow double that time.

farmlands in the Tianjin Province (four hours from Beijing), and you will run for four miles along the Great Wall itself.

www.great-wall-marathon.com

Safaricom Marathon (Lewa Wildlife Conserve, Kenya)

June, 650 runners

Every team entering is required to raise at least 100,000 Kenyan shillings (about $15,000) for conservation projects in the region. The course is set entirely in a game reserve, so you may find yourself racing giraffes or wildebeest, but it's a tough race over rugged terrain, in very hot conditions and at 5,500 feet above sea level. It's not unusual for Kenyans to take the first 30 or so places. Can't think why.

www.lewa.org/lewa_marathon.php

Easter Island

June, 150 runners

More than 2000 miles from any mainland, this recently inaugurated event is the world's most remote marathon. And you'll be reminded you are on one of the world's most mysterious places as the course affords views of some of the island's 800 moai, monolithic human-like statues carved out of hardened volcanic ash. Conservation concerns mean the race cannot run too close to them.

At the time of writing the Easter Island Marathon had no official website, but information and entry forms can be found at **www.marathontour.com/easterisland**

San Francisco

July, 15,000 runners

Taking in Fisherman's Wharf, Haight-Ashbury, the Golden Gate Bridge (views of and crossing), Golden Gate Park and the Mission district, this is a fabulous way to see the city. It is also probably the only marathon on the circuit to mark each mile with a specially commissioned picture by a local artist.

www.runsfm.com

Tip: Don't prepare for any marathon by scheduling in walking breaks, as this means you'll be approaching the start assuming you're not going to run the entire 26.2 miles. This, essentially, means you've undertrained to run the distance. Aim (and train) to run the whole course, and only walk as a fallback if you can't make it – you'll feel much more satisfied with your achievement.

the big 26.2

Tip: If you're tapering down for an overseas marathon, you might as well do it in an interesting foreign city, so travel to a race a few days beforehand. It'll also give you a better chance to acclimatise or get over jet lag.

Fact: Even if you're not running in a city's marathon, they are great events to attend as a spectator and worth considering when you plan your vacation dates.

Fact: Nothing beats that triumphant warrior feeling of cooling down decked out in your silver blanket and your medal. Everybody who has ever run a marathon is a hero, so don't be shy about it, make the most of your achievement – after my first London Marathon I wore my medal for three days!

Sydney

September, 20,000 runners

This was made much faster in 2006, when the gruelling Observatory Hill was replaced with a flatter final two miles. It still goes over Sydney Harbour Bridge and finishes in front of the Opera House.
www.sydneyrunningfestival.org

Le Marathon des Châteaux du Medoc

September/October, 8,000 runners

This passes through 59 vineyards in the Medoc region of France, including Château Lafite Rothschild and Château Mouton Rothschild, and aid stations will offer a choice of red or white as well as water. It's not for nothing this is billed as "The world's slowest marathon"!
www.marathondumedoc.com

Athens

November, 3,000 runners

Be a part of marathon history and run (more or less) the route that Phidippides ran when he carried news of that Athenian victory back in 490 BC. Just don't drop dead at the finish line. It's also the same route as run in the 2004 Olympic Games and takes you into the shadow of the Acropolis and to a finishing line in the city's Olympic stadium.
www.athensmarathon.com

Marathon de Monaco et des Riviera (Monte Carlo)

November, 2,200 runners

The only marathon on the circuit to go through three different countries – France, Italy and Monaco – the course runs past the glitz and glamour of the Riviera's promenade and up into the mountains above it for spectacular coastal views.
www.monaco-marathon.com

Not racing? Take a runner's holiday.

Running is the best way to get a snapshot view of whatever city you are staying in. If you're running in the early morning, it can feel like a real privilege to be up and about as that city is waking up and to be on the streets before they are jammed with traffic and pedestrians. An hour or so's run is also a brilliant way to discover interesting shops, old churches, odd-looking buildings or unusual parks, to come back and investigate fully when you are wearing proper clothes – I happened across Parc Monceau in Paris while on a run, and have been going back, fascinated by its statues and follies, ever since.

Of course you have to take a few basic precautions as it's easy to get lost or to stray from a safe area into one where it's not such a good idea to be a tourist out on your own. Ask in your hotel for recommended running routes and, if they involve negotiating more than one junction, write the directions down in a flow diagram.

Or you can go prepared. International runner's guide *RunCity* (**www.runcity.co.uk**) has a series of safe, central 10k runs in London, Paris and New York, with new cities being added. These runs, available as downloadable mp3 files, are all circular and will take you past a number of landmarks while providing historical information. The *Rough Guide* travel books (**www.roughguides.com**) all contain detailed maps of major cities' central areas, from which you can plan your own runs. However, it's worth confirming with somebody local that there will be no problems with your route.

> **Tip:** Check the weather conditions of wherever you are going to be racing and make sure you pack the appropriate running gear.

> **//** Running is the best way to orientate yourself when you go abroad. Get up early in a strange city or part of the countryside and go for a run – you'll get a much more accurate picture of where you are, what it's really like and what people actually do. **//**
> **Hugh Jones**

> **Tip:** If you are going away with business colleagues or on a company conference, persuade your co-workers to take their running shoes, or even buy a pair for the event.

r

Let's speak Runglish

The best way to feel like a runner is to sound like a runner, and for that you'll need fluent Runglish, which, by the way, also provides a handy glossary of terms used in this book.

Aerobic: Literally, "with oxygen". Aerobic exercise is of long duration and medium intensity, working the heart at around seventy per cent of its maximum capacity for at least twenty minutes, increasing the oxygen supply to muscles. It will improve cardiovascular fitness.

Anaerobic: Without oxygen. This sort of exercise is high-intensity stuff and powers the body explosively in the very short term by burning glycogen without oxygen.

Articular surfaces: The areas inside a joint that actually rub together.

Body Mass Index (BMI): A calculation based on height and weight that indicates how overweight you are. However, as it doesn't differentiate between muscle and fat, it can be misleading for muscular physiques.

Bonk: Sudden extreme fatigue caused by the emptying of glycogen reserves to fuel the muscles. Same as the wall, see below.

Cadence: The number of strides in a prescribed period of time, usually a minute – the same as Turnover, see below.

Carb loading: Increasing your energy reserves in the days before a race by eating more carbohydrates than you would normally.

Crosstraining: Adding exercises other than running into your training schedule.

Core strength: The power needed in your trunk to hold your body up correctly so that it provides the necessary fulcrums for the legs and arms.

Elastic recoil: The energy produced when stretched tendons and muscles snap back to their regular length, like rubber bands. Elastic recoil is a vital part of how efficiently your stride will carry you forward.

Fartlek: A training method that alternates aerobic and anaerobic exercise to build up intensity. In your case, it will mostly involve short sprints within your run with an increase in pace each time you go back to running. Invented in Sweden, fartlek translates as "speed play" and will improve cardiovascular levels and help develop speed and endurance.

Fast-twitch muscles: These contract faster and more explosively, are white in colour, have less resistance to fatigue and are used for anaerobic exercise. Sprinters and sportsmen who need short bursts of speed develop a greater proportion of fast-twitch muscles.

Foot drag: The movement of your striking foot as it is pushed backwards through the stride (in relation to your centre of gravity moving forwards).

Gait cycle: The contact made by the sole of your shoe with the ground as you run through a stride: the midfoot should hit first, rolling forward through the pronation (see below) to push off with the ball of the foot then on to the toes.

Glycogen: Fuel for the muscles stored in the muscles. It is a complex carbohydrate, obtained from eating starchy foods, and is the distance runner's best source of energy.

Glycolysis: The breaking down of carbohydrate in the bloodstream to provide energy for the body.

Interval training: Carefully calculated periods of high-intensity exercise alternated with resting "recovery" periods.

Kick: The sprint or speeding up at the end of a race.

Lactic acid/lactate: Although slightly different in chemical composition, both are the metabolic by-products of burning glycogen to power the muscles. For years believed to be the cause of post-run soreness and fatigue, they are now known to be a valuable additional energy source.

Lactate threshold: The point during intense exercise when your lactate production increases to a level at which it outstrips removal and the concentration of it in your bloodstream starts to rise.

Laddering: An increasingly intense speed-training session, in which each segment ups the tempo.

Overtraining: Not allowing sufficient recovery time between training sessions, resulting in cumulative chronic fatigue.

Pronation: The degree to which your foot rolls inwards or outwards as you go through the gait cycle.

Running economy: How efficiently you run, measured in the "cost" of your movement in terms of how much oxygen is required to run at different speeds. The figure is arrived at by measuring your VO_2 (see below) in relation to your body weight while running prescribed speeds.

Running splits: Splitting a course or a run into several different distance points – miles or kilometres, for instance – and recording your times for each section separately.

Skeletal muscles: Long, cylindrical muscles, attached to the skeleton (hence the name) that facilitate movement by contracting and relaxing. They are divided into fast-twitch and slow-twitch.

Slow-twitch muscles: Reddish in colour, these fibres are capable of storing more oxygen, have a slower contraction time and are more resistant to fatigue. Distance runners develop more slow-twitch muscles.

Tapering: Tailing off the amount and intensity of your training schedule as you get nearer race day.

Turnover: The number of strides in a prescribed period of time, usually per minute – the same as Cadence.

VO_2 (volume of oxygen): The amount of oxygen your system can transport and utilise during exercise, measured in either millilitres per kilogram of body weight per minute or litres per minute – this book uses the former.

VO_2 max: The maximum amount of oxygen your system can deliver while you are exercising. VO_2 max is taken as a measurement of a person's overall fitness levels.

The wall: The point during a long race when all the body's supplies of glycogen are used up and the muscles power themselves by burning fat. Because fat is a far less efficient fuel than glycogen this change over results in a dramatic fatigue – hitting the wall.

Index

index